HAL M. HELMS

ECHOES OF
eternity

Listening to the Father

PARACLETE PRESS
BREWSTER, MASSACHUSETTS

Unless otherwise designated, Scripture quotations are taken from the King James Version of the Bible.

Scripture quotations designated RSV are from the Revised Standard Version of the Bible, copyright 1946, 1952, 1971 by the Division of Christian Education of the National Council of the Churches of Christ in the USA. Used by permission.

Library of Congress Cataloging-in-Publication Data

    Echoes of eternity: listening to the Father.
    p. cm.
    ISBN 1-55725-173-8 (alk. paper)
    1. Devotional calendars. I. Paraclete Press.

BV4810.E24   1996
242'.2—dc20

    96-24801
    CIP

10 9 8 7 6 5 4 3 2 1

Published by Paraclete Press,
Brewster, Massachusetts
www.paracletepress.com
Printed in the United States of America

My prayer life has been "reborn"

FOR FIVE YEARS HAL HELMS' BOOKS have been the most important part of my day. They have taught me how to hear God's voice during my prayer times. I now come to the Father longing to hear Him speak.

Sally Russ
Menlo Park Presbyterian Church
Menlo Park, California

Courage to look to God

HERE IN THE CARE HOME, WHERE I LIVE, we have a great need for uplifting thinking. Through a friend I was introduced to *Echoes of Eternity*. One of the caregivers and I read it each day. *Echoes* gives me the courage to look to God, to listen for His voice, and to gain energy to enjoy the gift of each day.

Glenna Hopewell
Celeste Care Home
San Mateo, California

I HAVE BOTH VOLUMES AND THEY ALWAYS PROVIDE ME WITH A GOOD WORD at the appropriate time. That's the Holy Spirit. Just marvelous.

Donna Schuman
Florence, Massachusetts

A wonderful source

TWO MONTHS AGO ELIZABETH, MY WIFE OF ALMOST FIFTY YEARS, died after suffering nine years with ALS. Even after fifty-two years in the ministry, I was not prepared for such a loss. Our daughter loaned me a copy of *Echoes of Eternity*. During these difficult days the Scripture verses and the comments in this devotional guide have provided the strength and encouragement I needed.

Jerold R. McBride, Th.D.
Pastor Emeritus
First Baptist Church
San Angelo, Texas

Meets my immediate need every day

"DOES JESUS EVER SPEAK TO ME?" The closest I have ever come is *Echoes of Eternity*. I read it every day. It is so intimate and personal that it meets my immediate need.

Walt Gerber
Pastor Emeritus
Menlo Park Presbyterian Church
Menlo Park, California

A comforting word for a time of great need

Echoes of Eternity WAS PUBLISHED JUST BEFORE OUR WEDDING IN 1996. We gave copies of it to our out-of-town guests. The mother of my best friend from high school passed it on to her daughter and son-in-law, whose young son was dying of a brain tumor. They began reading from it every day. Their son died shortly thereafter, and they called to tell us how blessed they were by the reading from *Echoes* that day. "I am gathering unto Myself a people to dwell eternally with Me. Even now that dwelling is prepared, and your life span is preparation to fit you for it. . . . Do you see, My child, how My mercy covers all that happens, and that I am never far from you?"

Danielle Bushnell
Orleans, Massachusetts

Introduction

Talking and listening. Speaking and hearing. These are the fundamental prerequisites for conversation. Yet with most of us, our relation with our heavenly Father consists mostly of our speaking. Our oldest traditions, however, tell us that we are invited to hear as well as speak.

We do well to be cautious in this procedure. Our own wishes and the interference of other voices can drown out the "still, small voice," unless we arm ourselves against illusion, delusion and deception. We do well to be modest in our claims about what we have heard.

Yet having said all that, there is a wonderful invitation that stands as valid today as it was when it was spoken:

"If any one hears my voice and opens the door, I will come in to him and eat with him, and he with me. . . . He who has an ear, let him hear what the Spirit says to the churches." (Revelation 3:20b, 22 RSV)

What the Spirit has said to one who has listened is shared in the hope that these impressions will convey "what the Spirit says" to the hearts of those who read them and will encourage others to "open the door" to hear for themselves what the Spirit is saying.

Hal M. Helms
Chaplain of the Community of Jesus,
Orleans, Massachusetts
August, 1996

JANUARY

Lord, speak to me, that I may speak
    In living echoes of Thy tone;
As Thou hast sought, so let me seek
    Thine erring children lost and lone.

Frances R. Havergal
1836-1879

January First

Lord, Thou hast been our dwelling place in all generations.
Psalm 90:1 (RSV)

Have no fear for tomorrow, My child. Tomorrow will hold only what I bring or allow in your life. All your tomorrows are in My hand. I am the Lord of the years. My hand is a gracious hand and all My ways are faithfulness.

As long as you keep your eyes focused on minor pains and difficulties in your path, you rob yourself of the joy of My fellowship— the communion of the Holy Spirit. You are meant to walk in a different realm—the larger reality of My kingdom. This is not an imaginary "place." It is a present reality which is open to My children who seek and find it. Doubt and self-pity close off this reality from you, but they do not, cannot, destroy it. So seek and find, My child. Seek and find what hitherto you have only dimly grasped.

January Second

First be reconciled to thy brother, and then come and offer thy gift.
Matthew 5:24

Put away ill will. It corrodes and eats away the very foundation of your soul. Fight against the feelings of hurt and outrage, and turn every thought that would lead to ill will into prayer. You cannot hate and really pray for someone's good at the same time.

Realize, however, that it is primarily for your own sake that you are doing this. You must guard against further indulging in hateful thoughts and feelings—even repressed ones—and pray for *good* for those who hurt or oppose you. You see examples of what can happen to a soul who did not restrain feelings of hate and vengeance. Not a pretty sight, is it? Hatred and ill will are never pretty when fully unmasked. The pleasure you derive in them cannot be compared to the *joy* you will have when you put them away.

January Third

If Thou, Lord, shouldest mark iniquities, O Lord, who shall stand? But there is forgiveness with Thee, that Thou mayest be feared.
                                                        Psalm 130:3,4 (RSV)

Your fear of being wrong, My child, shows that you are not living by grace, but by "works." This is not a minor fault, but a major block in our relationship and in your spiritual growth. Go and read again Brother Lawrence's testimony—and let your heart absorb the truth of it.

Worry about what others may think of you, how they react to you, puts an obstacle between you and Me. No matter how pious you may appear to others, I see your heart, and I tell you again: your fear of being wrong shows that you are not living by grace. Your soul is filled with accusations against My goodness. Otherwise, there would be only a desire to please Me out of gratitude, not out of fear.

January Fourth

While ye have light, believe in the light, that ye may be the children of light.
John 12:36

Hark unto Me, My dear child, and listen attentively. Learn to look with the eyes of the spirit beyond the outward shell. Let your thoughts and your words aim at what lies hidden from the natural view, and do not be confused by it. I will give you the discernment you need in order to minister life. Remember that My love and care go beyond any immediate problem. Pray that you may see with Me the long view—the goal to which I am leading each child of Mine. Too much attention to each single incident can cloud that vision and cause unnecessary problems.

January Fifth

If it be possible, as much as lieth in you, live peaceably with all men.
Romans 12:18

My Spirit strives within to bring your spirit into harmony with My divine purposes. Often you are like a bird trapped or held in the hand—struggling to get "free"—to what? You do not know.

My Spirit strives to bring you into peace. You long for peace, but you do not know how to achieve it. Only My wisdom and My way can bring you into perfect peace—and for My way to prevail, your ways must be given up.

Marvel not that the striving between us often leaves you confused and unsatisfied. These are indications of your lack of full surrender. The dissatisfaction is the fruit of your hold-out at some level. But I am God, and My mercy does not abandon you to your false "victory." The fruit of it in your soul is meant to warn you that losing is winning, and winning is always losing.

January Sixth

If we live in the Spirit, let us also walk in the Spirit.

Galatians 5:25 (RSV)

I am caring for you, My child, I am caring for you. Remember, with Me there are no accidents, no surprises. What comes to you unexpectedly and unbidden has been long known and foreseen by Me. It comes by My permission and carries the seed of My blessing.

I bid you now to look up. Trust Me beyond your understanding and knowledge. Put your hand in My fatherly hand—to be guided into what lies ahead for you. Fear not and be not troubled. I am faithful, and will not leave or forsake you.

January Seventh

Rejoice in the Lord always: and again I will say, Rejoice.

Philippians 4:4

Praise is the best medicine, but praise must be from the right motive. It must not be thought of as a source of blessing and healing, even though they are its by–products. Praise must come from your gratitude for My many mercies, and for specific ones. Let it well up from your heart and unite with the universal song from all the ages past—an eternal alleluia. Let it drown out the little voices of woe and complaint that run around in your head. Let praise draw you out of concern with your physical condition—and thus foretaste My victory over them all. Praise is work for you, My child, because you have done so little of it in your life. Redeem the time you have left on earth—let your mouth and your heart be filled with My praise.

January Eighth

If ye keep my commandments ye shall abide in My love; even as I have kept My Father's commandments, and abide in His love.

John 15:10

Hear and obey. That is the key to your path of blessing. Hearing is not enough. The "birds of the air" pick up the seed sown "along the wayside." Thoughts, fears, and dreams travel along that way—

leaving precious little soul in which My word can take root and grow. Nourish that which lives. Treasure the words you have received, not as museum pieces to be admired, dusted, and stored—but as spiritual dynamos, sources of renewal, "jump-starters" when you have grown lax or weak.

Hear. Blessed are the ears attuned to My voice. Blessed are those in whose hearts are My ways.

Obey. Procrastination is but another form of disobedience. It is not neutral, but an active, corrosive evil. Watch it, and move against it at all costs.

January Ninth

Blessed be God, even the Father of our Lord Jesus Christ, the Father of mercies and the God of all comfort, who comforteth us in all our tribulation.

II Corinthians 1:3,4

Bring them to Me, My child, bring them to Me—the wounds of the past, the painful memories of foolish choices, the hurtful wrongs you inflicted on others—all that burdens your soul with sad regrets. It was for sinners that I came to this earth. It was for the undone, the heavy-laden souls who knew no relief from the pain of their wrongness.

The crucifixion you feel as these old memories return is a crucifixion of pride. The humiliation and shame are but necessary blows to the nature that still seeks to be "somebody." As you bury the memories in My wounds, there is no place for boasting or vainglory. Neither is there any reason to continue to nurture the pain. Gratitude, praise, and expectation can replace the defeating deadness of old regrets.

January Tenth

Before the mountains were brought forth, or ever Thou hadst formed the earth and the world, even from everlasting to everlasting, Thou art God.
Psalm 90:2

My word today is this: Endless. You see and fear the "ends." I see endlessness—eternity. You fear becoming nothing. I see your life growing and continuing. Come over to My viewpoint. See your life in this perspective. Do not grasp at the past nor the present. Let them go with the passing. They are not meant to last. But your life in Me is endless. New times, new challenges, new opportunities to know My ways better. Endless.

January Eleventh

Everyone that asketh receiveth.

Matthew 7:8

Ask and it will be given you. Be more bold in your asking, My child, for I take pleasure in granting the requests of My children.

Asking is a way of expressing your faith in Me and in My goodwill toward you. Take your eyes off the "impossibilities" of circumstances, and ask for what I put in your heart to ask. The process is vital to your maturing and deepening in faith.

Make a record of the big and small things you pray for, so that you will know the surety of what I am saying to you. Ask and believe!

January Twelfth

Look unto the rock whence ye are hewn, and to the hole of the pit whence ye are digged.

Isaiah 51:1

My child, do not despise the day of your beginnings. It was no accident or chance that you were born and brought up in your family. Do not be ashamed of them nor of their devotion. All My people are shaped by traditions they did not invent. You have carried into your present life some of the seeds of truth I planted long ago. In spite of your rebellion and sin, the seed remained. It will yet bear fruit to My glory.

Give thanks then, My child, for My fatherly care over you. Let the memories of the past give you courage and incentive for faithfulness in the present. Contemplate My goodness and the sweetness of My presence. In the secret place commune with Me, and do not be ashamed of the "homeliness" of your devotion. There is room for that, too, in My heart.

January Thirteenth

Make Thy face to shine upon Thy servant; and teach me Thy statutes.
Psalm 119:135 (RSV)

Behind the clouds, My glorious light. Behind the doubts, My sure promises. Behind the fears, My blessed hope. Let no darkness remain in your soul, My child. Let the light of My Spirit shine in its hidden places. Do not nourish dark and wicked thoughts, even for an instant. Their stain remains and pollutes. There is light behind the clouds, glorious light. Seek and find it and walk in it.

January Fourteenth

Behold, I have graven thee upon the palms of my hands; Thy walls are continually before me.

Isaiah 49:16

My child, I have told you, you are graven on My hand—My right hand. By this I meant to quell every fear and doubt you have about your life in Me. "He who fears is not perfected in love." That is a message to you in the first place, so that you bear in mind the inner work you must still do. Love is active, not passive—and you have become much, much too passive. Exercise your love—such as it is—so that it might fill a greater space in you. Stop quenching the Spirit and act on the intuitive thoughts that come to you. In loving your neighbor as yourself, you will drive out the overweening self-concern that characterizes your life. Since I remember you, you can afford to forget you. Make a stab at it today!

January Fifteenth

For he doth not afflict willingly nor grieve the children of men.
Lamentations 3:33

I tell you of very truth, I share the sorrow of your heart for those you love who walk in the darkness of this world. The pain you feel is only a minor portion of Mine, and there is no way to avoid the suffering. I know My plans for them, which you do not, but you can trust My infinite mercy and wisdom to act. In the meantime, without being frivolous and irresponsible, you can keep lifting them up to Me. Remember that "prayer availeth much."

All this will work together for good for you and for those for whom you are praying, and My glory will be seen. Nothing worthwhile comes without struggle and pain since sin entered My world. But in spite of it all, I still love My creation and My plans for it are good.

My dear child, rest in Me.

January Sixteenth

But we all, with open face beholding as in a glass the glory of the Lord, are changed into the same image from glory to glory. . . .

II Corinthians 3:18

My child, it is a continual wonder and surprise to you that I, the Lord of all creation, should deign to speak and commune with you, a creature of dust and time. Yet here I glorify Myself in a way that only those created in My image can experience and realize. Nor is My glory a selfish one, for in this communion of Spirit with spirit, your own human nature is lifted to a new level.

Your earthly life span will never exhaust nor solve the mystery you touch here. That is too deep and profound for your present state. But it will "unfold" as you practice it, growing brighter and more precious, even as the mystery remains.

Take seriously this word: you are being prepared for the life beyond your earthly time-span. That is *real*. Do not lose sight of it nor waste the opportunities I am supplying you day by day.

January Seventeenth

. . . let us lay aside every weight, and the sin which doth so easily beset us, and let us run with patience the race that is set before us.

Hebrews 12:1

The riches of My kingdom are for the poor. They are hidden from those who come laden with their own gifts. That is why, My child, you are required to wait while we strip from you the weight of your internal wealth. Each time you are required to wait for My inner voice, you become aware anew of your own poverty of spirit. You face the deadness of your soul apart from My quickening power—and the suffering opens you to be blessed by My refreshing grace.

O ye of little faith! When will you learn to take each moment as it comes without faltering or whining at what it might turn out to be? Your lack of trust is a great handicap, and it is organically tied with your "inner wealth" which turns out to be dust and ashes. The riches of My kingdom are for the poor.

January Eighteenth

There shall no evil befall thee, neither shall any plague come nigh thy dwelling.

Psalm 91:10

"There shall no evil befall thee, neither shall any plague come nigh thy dwelling." The prayers of others have often shielded you, though you knew nothing about it. The faithfulness of others has formed an easier path for you to follow. Be faithful, then, My child, in your watch. Hold up those for whom I have given you responsibility. Link your prayers with the faithful around and before you—that My will may be accomplished "on earth as it is in heaven."

You still have much to learn about the mystery and marvel and might of prayer. These things are hidden from the wise, but are made known to "babes and sucklings"—to those who are small in their own eyes and are teachable.

January Nineteenth

I will lift up mine eyes unto the hills, from whence cometh my help.

Psalm 121:1

Fix your eyes on the far mountains—mountains of hope. The lowlands breed despair unless you raise your eyes and your mind above the immediate problem. Inspiration is an infilling of Spirit—your emptiness and lack filled up with what you can neither see nor understand. Yet it causes *substantial* change.

My work is not completed in a day. This is why I say, "Look to the far mountains." The delays you experience will be much easier to bear when you keep this in mind. I am working My purpose out. I am not asleep. I am not oblivious to you or your prayers. As long as you keep your hope alive, you will find everything needful for your journey of faith.

January Twentieth

. . . and he went out, not knowing whither he went.

Hebrews 11:8

I am the Lord your God. As Abraham walked with Me, so I bid you. Your heritage, like his, exceeds your imagination. Like Abraham, you must allow your family to choose to separate themselves from you. All is not lost! I am still the Lord. I put your prayers and longing in your heart for them, and expect you to be faithful. But it must be praying, not pulling—intercession, not intervention.

The work of prayer is your most important task. Do not neglect it nor make light of it. Prayer taps the infinite resources reserved for those who ask, seek, and knock. Have I not told you?

January Twenty–first

And there shall in no wise enter into it any thing that defileth, neither whatsoever worketh abomination, or maketh a lie: but they which are written in the Lamb's book of life.

Revelation 21:27

As the sun shines on the earth bringing light and unveiling the darkness, so does My Spirit shine upon your soul. Dark recesses are hidden from your consciousness, but they are not hidden from Me. The cleansing, purifying work of light must go on to prepare you for your eternal home. "And there shall in no wise enter into it anything that defileth." So the cleansing is an important part of your preparation.

Fear not this process, My child. Already you know that each step brings release and greater freedom within. There are still "ties that bind" and keep you from a full realization of My perfect work, but do not despair nor grow discouraged. *That* would only slow down the process. Be honest with yourself and seek the Spirit of Truth in facing all accusations. He convicts, cleanses, and sets free.

January Twenty–second

. . . avoiding profane and vain babblings, and oppositions of science falsely so called.

I Timothy 6:20

My word is often turned aside because it appears too simple. I come to you in simplicity in order to cut across the false reasoning you have allowed to grow up over many years. You come to me and complain of feeling dead and empty. Yet, truth to tell, you are full of many things—mainly yourself. Emptying out results in your feeling less empty.

Keep it simple today, My child. Do not yield to the temptation to try to appear profound. I know the way you should walk, so let Me guide and lead.

January Twenty–third

I am the Good Shepherd, and know My sheep, and am known of Mine.

John 10:14

I am the Good Shepherd. I know My sheep and am known of Mine. I have known you since you were conceived in your mother's womb, and have watched over you with tender care.

Why would you doubt My care for you? I did not bring you this far to abandon you! But My ways are not your ways and you still have much to learn of Me. Your knowledge and your faith are very small. I watch you draw back into yourself, rather than boldly coming out into the sunshine of My love.

January Twenty–fourth

This is the day which the Lord hath made; we will rejoice and be glad in it.
Psalm 118:24

The day is Mine. All things are held together by My power and will. "The earth is the Lord's and the fullness thereof, the world and they that dwell therein." The grandeur of this vision can bring light and hope into your dark day.

The day is Mine. I am the Light of the world and the Light of My people in a peculiar sense. I am your Light, My child, casting away the lingering shadows of doubt and sin. Light and health are closely related, as more light drives out the breeding places of sickness in your soul. You see and feel the bodily sickness, the ravages of disorder and disharmony in the flesh. I see the soul even more ravaged by dark thoughts and wrong attitudes. The soul struggles to live, but it needs My light and healing even more than does your bodily flesh.

The day is Mine. The light shines in the darkness, and the darkness cannot overcome it. Be of good cheer!

January Twenty–fifth

Fret not thyself because of evildoers, neither be thou envious against the workers of iniquity.

Psalm 37:1

Be not troubled in spirit over the negative things being bandied about. In very truth I tell you, the spirit of Antichrist is abroad and doing much harm among those open to it. It need not trouble you. Rather let it signal your need to draw closer to Me, your peace and your vindication. Did I not come to Job's defense after I had dealt with his self-righteousness? Did I not promise that those who follow Me would know persecution? This, My child, is but *reality*. It is built into the fallen state of this world. Until all is brought into conformity with My divine, creative purpose, conflict and persecution *will* be the lot of those who walk with Me.

But is it not a good walk, My child?

January Twenty–sixth

For we walk by faith, not by sight.

II Corinthians 5:7

Do not fret yourself with things too high for you—with concerns over which you have no control. Such fretting only robs you of peace and wastes energy. Focus on the things for which you are sent. Don't fritter away the days and hours with idleness. Claim the high calling I have given you, and quit yourself like a man.

Those who walk with Me must sometimes walk in shadows. You must be prepared for silence as well as speech. I do not always explain what I am doing, and I want your unqualified trust in Me. If everything were absolutely clear, you would be walking by sight, and for My own reasons, I have called you to the walk of faith. Faith grows in the shadows, but shrinks in the light. You will understand this better when all becomes clear. In the shadows, practice praise. Go steadily on the path I have laid out for you, and be of good cheer.

January Twenty–seventh

And the light shines in the darkness, and the darkness has not overcome it.
John 1:5

The day has dawned with the light of My love. Darkness cannot hold it back because I am its light. Your fears about the future are futile, for the future is in My hand. Every time you give way to foreboding, you abandon the faithground I have provided for you. My dear child, can you stop loving your children? Neither can I stop loving Mine. It is My nature to love, and so I counsel you again: leave the future to Me—your future and your loved ones' future. I care, and will care. Be at peace.

Go forward into the day without fear. I go before you and prepare your way. There are no surprises for Me in the events of the day, even though they may surprise or even startle you. Keep your perspective. Do not allow the enemy to gain a stronghold through your imagination. Let the truth be your shield and buckler. Remember, My child, you are Mine and the day is Mine.

January Twenty–eighth

For we are saved by hope.

Romans 8:24

Cast not away your hope, My child, for I am its source and its fulfillment. It is I who put hope in your heart, and those who hold fast their hope shall not be confounded. The fractured image of reality you now see will one day be replaced by a clear, undistorted vision. You cannot see the whole picture, but what you see is enough.

January Twenty–ninth

But though He cause grief, yet will He have compassion according to the multitude of His mercies.

Lamentations 3:32

In the shadow of My hand, pain. In the touch of My hand, healing. Sometimes the shadow lingers and pain is prolonged. Will you trust Me in the shadow as well as the sun? Can you walk with Me over rough ways and not complain? Comfort is a fleeting thing. Struggle brings inner strength. I do not want you to be consumed with attention on the difficulties of your life. They are yet minor in comparison with what many are called to endure. Rather choose to believe that shadows pass. My good will prevails, and your feeble faith is not in vain.

January Thirtieth

Thus saith the One whose name is Holy: I dwell in the high and holy place, with him also that is of a contrite and humble spirit.

Isaiah 57:15

I have told you before, and I tell you again. You must not seek honor and recognition. Your service to Me must be free from the demand of reward. This craving, even when repressed and unconscious, binds you, blinds you, and closes your ears to My voice.

Do you not sense your emptiness and deadness when I am withdrawn from you? That can be and should be a useful reminder that you are not the creator or originator of all good things. They all flow from Me, and you are allowed to be the instrument by which they are expressed. That in itself is blessing enough!

January Thirty–first

Before I was afflicted I went astray; but now have I kept Thy word.
Psalm 119:67

My child, do not despise My chastenings. They are sent for your ultimate good, painful and difficult as they are for you. I have not forgotten to be gracious, and I am not absent from any trial you are being asked to endure. As Abraham found, My eye is upon you, and when the work is done, My answer is there, waiting to be revealed.

The secret of the Lord is with them that fear Him. This holy fear is a protection against that part of your nature that would carry you into complete darkness. Cherish it, and tremble before My Word. Cherish it, and let it be a protection to you, like a wall around a sheltered garden. You will come to know and trust Me more and more if you will not despise My chastenings.

FEBRUARY

I come to the garden alone,
    While the dew is still on the roses;
And the voice I hear, ringing on my ear,
    The Son of God discloses;

And He walks with me, and He talks with me,
    And He tells me I am His own.
And the joy we share as we tarry there,
    None other has ever known.

C. Austin Miles
1868-1946

February First

O come, let us worship and bow down; let us kneel before the Lord our Maker.

Psalm 95:6 (RSV)

The bowed head and contrite heart are fitting as you wait for My word. They are fitting, too, before the circumstances I will to place in your path. Your head does not bow easily—for you still long to be in charge. Little do you realize the hold that desire has on your life, and the peace you forfeit as a result. Esau despised his birthright for a mess of pottage. You forfeit yours for less!! O My dear child, learn to bow the head. Learn to bow the heart! My way truly is best.

February Second

Unto the upright there ariseth light in the darkness; He is gracious, and full of compassion, and righteous.

Psalm 112:4

Light arises in the darkness for those who love Me. No threat can thwart the ongoing fulfillment of My will. Say to those of a fearful heart: Behold your King! Have I failed you in the past? Has My help been withheld from your cry? Let everything conspire to propel you forward in the path I have laid out for you. No, you cannot see the distant end—but there is light on your path today. Keep your eye on the light, and the darkness will lose its power to trouble you.

February Third

And when He [the Comforter] is come, He will convict the world of sin, and of righteousness, and of judgment.

John 16:8

I come not to praise you nor condemn you, but to build you up in spirit. Your adversary would use both praise and condemnation to confound you and tear you down. The memory of past sins should not linger, but hasten you to thankfulness for forgiveness and mercy. The sobering result of reminders of your wrong choices should keep you from vainglory. Remembering who you are is not a cause for despair but wonder. My presence in your life has saved you from many disasters—so let them remind you that your help has been, is, and ever shall be from Me.

February Fourth

Take My yoke upon you and learn of Me.

Matthew 11:29

Take My yoke upon you and learn of Me. Learn. Learn. You know so little, and have so far to go! You tell others of My glory and My grace, but inwardly know precious little of either. O My child, how often would I have led you in paths of righteousness, and you would not! Another master would have grown weary and impatient, but I am "slow to anger and of great mercy." I have had to bring suffering into your life because your proud and haughty nature would not otherwise bend. Do you think this was a joy to Me, to see you broken and sick? No, for I am afflicted in the affliction of My people. But I did look for positive results—and in part they came. But only in part. The proud and arrogant person still lives—subdued somewhat—but far from dead!

My yoke—My restraining and guiding Hand, the harness of My call—these are your safeguards and through the restraint of that yoke you are learning of Me. Learn! Listen and learn! Do this, My child, for the sake of My love for you.

February Fifth

All Mine are Thine, and Thine are Mine; and I am glorified in them.

John 17:10

All are Mine—the living and the dead. Those who have gone from your sight and left their bodies to return to dust—still live in My sight. You are connected with the unseen world with ties that were made during their earthly life span. You are never alone in that sense, My child.

You have tended to think of your life as a solo performance. That is a grave misunderstanding. Whenever you can you should strengthen the inner sense of connectedness with your companions. Loneliness is not inevitable. Once you catch the vision of being part of the great company, not imaginary or mystical, but *real*, you will begin to experience the benefits I planned in My divine scheme of things. Don't be afraid of "the company of heaven," My child. It is *real* and you are called to be part of it one day.

February Sixth

And God saw everything that He had made, and behold it was very good.

Genesis 1:31

I am He who gives existence to all things. It is My overflowing love expressed in My universe—My creation. You exist because of

My desire to share My life with others. When My love reaches your hearts, and you begin to love Me and one another, then My creative purpose is being fulfilled. It is My will that there be a creation moved by and filled with love. You call it "heaven." It is the Home toward which I am leading you. You have only "tasted" it thus far—there is far more.

February Seventh

And they heard the voice of the Lord God walking in the garden in the cool of the day.

Genesis 3:8

I have walked and talked with many a soul over the years. Yet surprisingly few of My people understand and avail themselves of this privilege. It was My first plan, as revealed in the Garden of Eden, to have fellowship with those I had created in My image. Then misuse of the freedom. Which, that image carried with it meant a loss on both sides—and the possibility had to be re-established. You catch glimpses of it in the Old Testament writings, for there were, even then, those who discovered and claimed this fellowship.

I came in full measure with the gift of the Holy Spirit, poured out on My people. The veil of the temple was rent, and access—an open door—placed for the highest and lowest among them.

Still even My own seem to prefer distance to nearness. They erect new barriers and place new conditions and restrictions on this invitation to fellowship. You are required to continue to struggle against the willful and rebellious nature that seeks to deafen your ears to My voice. Practice instant obedience to My Spirit's "nudges"—the gentle voice you so often ignore. This will put you "on track" to have a closer walk with Me.

February Eighth   2 . 8 . 2020

Let us therefore come boldly unto the throne of grace, that we may obtain mercy, and find grace to help in time of need.

Hebrews 4:16

My dear child, know that I love you. You long to be loved and yet you are afraid of love, and close your heart against Me and those who seek admission. You *need* My love, not just as an objective reality—which it is—but as a subjective, inner heart experience, which you do not, for the most part, have. I say this not to condemn you, but to invite you to open the door that I may comfort and sustain you in your times of need.

February Ninth

Except the Lord build the house, they labor in vain that build it; except the Lord keep the city, the watchman waketh but in vain.

Psalm 127:1

Unless I build the house, their labor is vain who build it. Unless I guard the city, the watchmen wait in vain. It is not just to the generation to whom those words first came, but to yours that I send them. Beware of the arm of flesh. Beware of leaning on human wisdom and worldly means. Be as wise as serpents and as harmless as doves. You are in danger of being seduced by human reasoning—reducing your dependence on My sovereign power and wisdom. Caution is needed and much prayer that you will see, find, and follow the right path.

February Tenth

Deep calleth unto deep at the noise of Thy waterspouts: all Thy waves and Thy billows are gone over me.

Psalm 42:7

Heart to heart, and Spirit to spirit, our fellowship does not always need words. When you are at peace in My presence, know that I am communing with you. And when words fail you in prayer, remember that the Spirit searches the heart and prays with groanings that are to you, wordless. I am ever ready to hear the cry of need and the voice of genuine praise.

February Eleventh

Pray for the peace of Jerusalem: they shall prosper that love thee.
Psalm 122:6

My child, put away the negative thoughts and feelings that are so readily in your head. They are death to the life I am giving you, and they eat away like acid your soul. When the accusing and judgmental thoughts arise, quickly turn the person or situation over to Me in prayer. Defeat the ploy of the enemy with a weapon he cannot touch. Pray for the peace of Jerusalem. That is, bring every concern into the realm of My peace and power, believing and trusting that I can make all things work together for the good of all concerned.

I challenge you to put this into practice faithfully, for you cannot yet imagine the blessing it will bring you. I want you to be a channel of blessing, not of cursing.

February Twelfth

Men ought always to pray, and not to faint.

Luke 18:1

My dear child, I quicken dead souls to new life. Your own feeling of deadness is a necessary preparation to help you receive and recognize My coming.

You wonder why you have not made more progress in your prayer life. It is because you do not yet want this more than you want other things. You still have a desire for power—power to change things according to your understanding. For your own sake, My child, I have not allowed this. Say "No" to it, painful as it feels. Learn from others how they have given it up. Come with Me into the place of yieldedness— for only there will you enjoy the "quickened" life My presence brings.

February Thirteenth

Though I have the gift of prophecy, and understand all mysteries and all knowledge, and though I have all faith, so that I could remove mountains, and have not charity, I am nothing.

I Corinthians 13:2

My word brings joy, even when it causes pain. It brings life, even when it brings death to your wonted ways. Rather, it brings joy *because* it brings pain, and life *because* it brings death.

The deepest things of life remain a mystery to you, My child, and it must be so. In the mystery there are realities as yet only faintly grasped or dimly seen. But their presence assures you that there is more to life with Me than you have yet experienced.

Do not be afraid of the mysteries, and do not try to explain them away. This foolish effort on your part has robbed you of blessings and stunted your growth in Me for many years. Expand the capacity of your soul to admit what you cannot understand or reason out— and let My word bring the life and joy you so much want and need.

February Fourteenth

We know that the whole creation groaneth and travaileth in pain together until now.

Romans 8:22

Yes, My child, the world is full of pain and suffering. Think not that I have forgotten it, or that My heart is unmoved by the cries of My children. It is not for you to understand My ways and My delays. It is for you to keep on looking to Me for *your* daily needs, and to be faithful in holding up the bundle of concerns I have laid on your heart.

One day your eyes will be opened to see what is now hidden from your view. In the meantime, do not turn your heart away from the suffering you see in this world. Turn every sight of pain and hurt into prayer. Learn to transform the pain into petition, knowing that I am at work to bring good out of every evil.

February Fifteenth

They shall lift up their voice, they shall sing for the majesty of the Lord.
                                                                    Isaiah 24:14

The curtains of your mind have been partially drawn back, My child, to give you a vision of the greatness and grandeur of My kingdom. "From the rising of the sun to the going down of the same"—"as far as East is from West"—"from generation to generation"—these are some of the divinely inspired descriptions of that greatness.

You need to bathe your soul in the vision, for your faith has been dwarfed, too encased in the timidity of your own heart. When I open your eyes to see, even briefly, what a great heritage you have, you must grasp and hold on to the larger reality. It will help you in fighting the extreme self-centeredness of your old nature.

February Sixteenth

Search me, O God, and know my heart: Try me, and know my thoughts:
And see if there be any wicked way in me.

Psalm 139:23,24 (RSV)

I am your Sun, your everlasting Light. When your heart is turned toward Me, My light illumines your soul. There you see many faults, many wounds, much that is not beautiful. This must be, My child, because the work is not yet complete. You cannot expose yourself to My light without this consequence. Your prayer, "see if there be any wickedness within me," is fulfilled each time you allow My light to shine in your heart.

Just as the sunlight destroys that which lives in darkness on this earth, the sunlight of My presence does its work in your soul. And so, though there is still much to do, and the faults and wounds are many, the healing and cleansing are going on and will go on as you turn your heart to My light.

February Seventeenth

That He might sanctify and cleanse [the church] with the washing of water by the word.

Ephesians 5:26

The cleansing of the soul is a long process. The stain of sin goes very deep, and surface cleansing is only part of the process. You get discouraged that old sinful thoughts and temptations keep "coming back." You are to learn to fight their early appearance more aggressively. Bring them to Me, My child, for you cannot handle them alone. Confess—do not deny nor repress—but confess them and place them under My cleansing blood. "Sinners washed beneath this flood lose all their guilty stains." This is an ongoing work of My grace, and I expect your full participation if you want to be prepared for the light I have in store for you "and for all who have loved My appearing."

February Eighteenth

And now abideth faith, hope, love, these three; but the greatest of these is love.

I Corinthians 13:13

My light and My truth, My child, are given according to your willingness and your ability to receive it. I am Light and I am

Truth—so light and truth are never wanting in your dealings with Me—never wanting from My side of the relationship.

You mingle that light and truth with the darkness, so it does not shine in its purity and clarity. Although you are concerned about the distortions others may cause, you are not concerned enough about your own. Your perceptions of Truth are not always accurate. You know the truth of that from the changes in perception that have come over the years. But at each stage, you tend to believe that you no longer "see through a glass darkly," and are too confident of your own "accurate" version. I do not want you to become wishy-washy, "ready to change" instantly. I want you to *desire* fuller light and more truth—more of Me and less of the opinions by which you inwardly rise above others. Hold the truth you have, My child, even what you *think* you have. But hold it with the sure knowledge that you yet see and know only in part. And long for, desire, pray for, and seek a fuller grasp of the Truth. Don't be afraid to let go the dark shadows of opinion, to let the light that is in you shine brighter—to your good and to My glory.

February Nineteenth

Let us therefore come boldly unto the throne of grace, that we may obtain mercy, and find grace to help in time of need.

Hebrews 4:16

My dear child, whenever you come to Me in prayer, whatever condition your soul may be in, come boldly and with full confidence. Drawing back, for whatever reason, is a form of rejection of Me and My love. False humility has no place in this relationship. I know you better than you know yourself. If I had put our relationship on the basis of your deserving, it would never have begun. So, in the words of My Word, "come boldly to the throne of grace that you may find help in the time of need."

February Twentieth

There is no fear in love; but perfect love casteth out fear.

I John 4:18

This is My word for today: just as love casts out fear, fear casts out love. You cannot love when fear is in control. You are not fighting your fear-filled thoughts hard enough. You too readily give ground to them. I bid you to remember—remember where you have been and what I have brought you through. Remember and rejoice—even when you can't see how things are going to work out in the present.

February Twenty–first

According to your faith be it unto you.

Matthew 9:29

Your trouble in receiving, My child, is your trouble in believing. Not only these words that I give you day by day, but many other gifts I would freely bestow in answer to childlike faith. "The simple heart that *freely* asks in love, receives."

I seek a people who are not afraid to believe boldly. History is a record of My faithful response to this kind of bold praying. I see instead, the tendency to rely on human schemes and worldly wisdom—and there is not simple, bold faith in that. So My blessing is delayed or its magnitude is diminished. "According to your faith be it unto you."

I set "impossible" goals before you to prove My power and goodness. You say, "They shall abundantly utter the memory of Thy great goodness." Why? Because they were faced with their own limits and My limitless goodness. Think on these things today, My child, and grow *more* simple.

February Twenty–second

Every good gift and every perfect gift is from above, and cometh down from the Father of lights, with whom is no variableness, neither shadow of turning.

James 1:17

My way is perfect and My love is pure. Your love is sullied with self-interest. It cannot be otherwise at this stage of growth. Only let there be growth, My child, growth away from all that the "natural you" implies—jealous, fearful, controlling, unmerciful—and let My spirit control and guide what you shall yet be.

In Me there is no variableness, neither shadow of turning. All is light. All is known. All is life. The mystery, My child, which you find in thinking of Me, is a mystery of light, not darkness. The greatest mystery you can contemplate is the mystery of My love— "love to the loveless shown." Think often of that. Let the theme of it soften your heart and your thought of others, especially those who do not yet see the wonder and glory of it all.

February Twenty–third

The light of the body is the eye: if therefore thine eye be single, thy whole body shall be full of light.

Matthew 6:22

The eye is a precious gift. It allows the manifold wonders and beauty of the created world to enter your mind and soul. You are *spiritually* affected by what the eye sees. And herein lies a problem. Your mind is not disciplined to focus on the inner vision. It grabs what the eye conducts to it and runs in many directions, always ending in *self*. This makes it a serious distraction, and is one of the reasons for praying with *closed* eyes. Even this is not a sure shield against distraction, for your mind will still process images stored in its memory.

Do not despair, My child, but do not accept this condition as unchangeable. Keep working at getting the inner vision calm, stable, and stayed on Me. It will not be easy, but nothing worthwhile comes without struggle.

February Twenty–fourth

Ye also helping together by prayer for us . . .

II Corinthians 1:11

My child, do not delay in coming to Me with every situation you face. Your life—your whole life—is in My care. Nothing happens or can happen outside that care. This is hard for you to grasp because you have allowed strongholds of unbelief to be built up in your soul. I said to My disciples when they asked the reason for their failure to exorcise the lunatic boy, "Because of your unbelief." Faced with that situation and My absence, their faith failed them. And they were powerless. But there was another failure. "This kind goes forth only by prayer." They were lacking in prayer.

Your strength and the inspiration and energy you need to fulfill your duties are dependent on your "prayer connection." That is why I say, "Do not delay in coming to Me in every situation you face." Prayer will make a difference, but it must be *practiced* to work.

February Twenty–fifth

Thus saith the Lord, In an acceptable time I have heard thee, and in a day of salvation I have helped thee.

Isaiah 49:8

None ever called on Me in vain. None. Though they knew Me not, though they may never have realized that their cry was heard, their call was not in vain. My ears are open to the cries of all My children, and My heart is open to their needs. Think not that I am unmoved at the sight of the suffering in the world.

Today I give you this word: Trust Me in all things. Everything is in My hands, and you can leave to Me whatever is disturbing or troublesome to you. Trust Me and seek to live in My peace.

February Twenty–sixth

We look not at the things which are seen, but at the things which are not seen; for the things which are seen are temporal; but the things which are unseen are eternal.

II Corinthians 4:18

Turn your eyes away from the drabness of the day and look at the brightness of My dwelling. I dwell in the high and holy place— and that means that where I am there is all the brightness and beauty you could desire. And I dwell with those who are of lowly and contrite hearts—which means that My beauty and glory will be yours to the extent that you have a contrite heart.

February Twenty–seventh

Verily I say unto you, If ye have faith as a grain of mustard seed, ye shall say unto this mountain, Remove hence to yonder place; and it shall remove; and nothing shall be impossible unto you.

Matthew 17:20

Oceans and mountains are no problem for Me. Harder it is to work a change in the human heart. Not only does sin cling closely to the heart—the heart clings closely to its sin. You experience the same old aches and longings, My child, and are lazy in your struggle to be free of them. Struggle you must, because I will not violate your will and do it for you. I *will* give you the grace and strength you need, and I want you to be free of them. It *can* take place—if your heart will let go.

February Twenty–eighth

Provide yourselves bags which wax not old, a treasure in the heavens that faileth not, where no thief approacheth, neither moth corrupteth. For where your treasure is, there will your heart be also.

Luke 12:33,34

Traveling along the road of your pilgrimage, there are lessons to be learned every day. There are old ties to be cut or loosened, so they will have no power to hold you back on your journey toward Me. Remember, My child, that is where your journey leads, toward Me— your true End and Home. All these earthly scenes are passing ones. They change constantly because that is their nature. They serve their purpose, but they are not the End. Mourn if you must the loosening ties, but do not linger long in tears. I am your Comforter and abiding Joy. Abide in Me.

February Twenty–ninth

But one thing is needful: and Mary hath chosen that good part, which shall not be taken away from her.

Luke 10:42

My child, you have chosen the better part. I say this to encourage you, not to puff you up in your own mind. You and I know who and what you are in yourself. But My grace has prevailed to give you a holy desire not to let that nature prevail. The better part requires a discipline you have yet to master. It requires a steadiness you have not yet achieved. Yes, achieved, for it is My plan and My gracious provision to allow you to *achieve* and be blessed through it. This is why passivity before the many assaults to your souls is so wrong. It is an ungodly surrender, an unnecessary one. I will show you how to fight, and will prompt you when the enemy comes—only be ready to follow through with Me in the battle.

MARCH

Horatius Bonar
1808-1889

I heard the voice of Jesus say,

"Come unto Me and rest;
Lay down, thou weary one, lay down
   Thy head upon My breast."
   I came to Jesus as I was,
Weary and worn and sad,
   I found in Him a resting-place
And He has made me glad.

I heard the voice of Jesus say,
   "Behold, I freely give
The living water, thirsty soul,
   Stoop down and drink and live."
I came to Jesus and I drank
   Of that life-giving stream;
My thirst was quenched, my soul revived,
   And now I live in Him.

I heard the voice of Jesus say,
   "I am this dark world's Light;
Look unto Me, thy morn shall rise,
   And all thy day be bright."
I looked to Jesus and I found
   In Him my Star, my Sun;
And in that light of life I'll walk,
   Till traveling days are done.

March First

Keep me as the apple of the eye, hide me under the shadow of Thy wings.

Psalm 17:8

My child, My child, why do you doubt My love? It grieves My heart for you to question the ways of My Providence. Have I not been with you in every dark place? Has there ever been an end to My amazing grace? Trust then; the future is all in My hands. The wind and the waves still obey My commands. Nothing shall touch you but by My permission. Relax and be still: that is My commission.

March Second

For the fruit of the Spirit is in all goodness and righteousness and truth.
Ephesians 5:9

Stand in truth. Seek the truth and pursue it. Flee from fantasies and falsehoods; the "icing" on the cake of deceit. Truth often cuts, sometimes wounds, but only to heal. Do not fear the truth. Stand in it boldly. Speak it courageously, even when it threatens a false peace. Know that I, the Lord, am the God of truth. Know that I, the Son of God, am the Truth embodied in a human life. Respect the truth, nay, reverence and honor it—for the truth brings life.

March Third

Blessed are the merciful, for they shall obtain mercy.

Matthew 5:7

Have mercy, My child, on those who have offended you. Remember how many times you have offended Me. My way is not the grudge-bearing way, but the forgiving way. I have called you in righteousness to walk a holy way—a way that leads to life abundant, full and free. That is the prize I call you to seek. Seek it with all your heart and pay any price it may demand. Do not hate the instruments I choose to crucify your pride. Pride is the enemy—not the poor human who has offended.

March Fourth

Ye do well that ye take heed, as unto a light that shineth in a dark place, until the day dawns and the daystar arise in your hearts.

II Peter 1:19

I move through the thickets of your thoughts, a ray of light and truth for your soul. Your thoughts weave a thicket of darkness— twisted, tangled, leading nowhere. My light and My truth lead you outward and onward. Do not drag the thicket with you. I will help you cut loose from the old patterns of desire and ambition. Believe Me, My child, it *can* happen if you are willing. But it must be sought and desired. Look for the light shining through the thicket and follow where it leads.

March Fifth

Redeeming the time, because the days are evil.

Ephesians 5:16

Quench not the Spirit when He prays within you. Remember, My child, that He searches all things and makes intercession according to My will. You do not know the extent of your need or the needs of others. Your prayers still lack the intensity of importunity. But the Spirit knows and bears your burden, waiting for you to comprehend. So do not despise My provisions for your welfare and for the welfare of those for whom you pray. Trust the Spirit's interceding cry, and do not quench His gift to you.

March Sixth

Even so, every good tree bringeth forth good fruit; but a corrupt tree bringeth forth evil fruit. Wherefore, by their fruits ye shall know them.

Matthew 7:17,20

The tree does not know how the fruit is made or what its end will be. Its task is to *be* and to send its roots deep into the soil. So with you, My child. It is not your care to be concerned about what will become of the "fruit" of your life. Keep sending the roots into the fertile soil of My Word, and into the living water of My Spirit. The fruit will be good and it will bless others. That is all you need to know—or can afford to know.

March Seventh

Yea, I have loved thee with an everlasting love; therefore with loving-kindness have I drawn thee.

Jeremiah 31:3

From My mouth My Word goes forth to bring life to the world. This world which I created, I created in love. It is still My world. My love is eternal. My love is infinite. My love is life-giving. My Word is My love. Hear My Word and live. Receive My Word and give. Give up the ways of death that life may blossom forth in all its abundance. Do you not see? Life for death. That is what My love offers—not once for all, but a daily, moment by moment exchange: My life for your death. My way for your way. This is what My love offers My world—and you, My child.

March Eighth

In that day shall the branch of the Lord be beautiful and glorious, and the fruit of the earth shall be excellent and comely for them that are escaped of Israel.

Isaiah 4:2

This, My child, is My promise to you—if you obey My voice and walk in the paths I lay out for you. My will is life—not darkness and death. You can still bring forth fruit unto My praise. Only redeem the time! Do not fritter away these precious days as though they will last forever. Claim the grace I offer and bear fruit for eternity.

March Ninth

And this is life eternal, that they might know thee the only true God, and Jesus Christ whom thou hast sent.

John 17:3

I am the Lord your God who dwells in you, nearer than breath itself. I am your life and the meaning of your life. This is life, to know Me and Jesus Christ whom I have sent. Set your affections on Me—and where I am, there you will be also. When your heart goes out for the things of this world, you reap unto yourself a harvest of deadness. I would that you have an abundant harvest of living fruit—life-bringing fruit that will bless others and glorify Me. The key is here: set your affections on Me.

March Tenth

And He arose and rebuked the wind, and said unto the sea, Peace, be still.

Mark 4:39

Peace, be still! Let the waves of uncertainty and fear subside. Know that I am with you, and will carry you through every trial. Peace, be still, and learn to trust where you cannot see.

March Eleventh

For it pleased the Father that in Him should all fullness dwell; and having made peace through the blood of the cross, by Him to reconcile all things unto Himself.

Colossians 1:19,20

In this sign you will conquer. In My cross is your victory. Mine is a finished work. Mine is a perfect work. And it is yours, My child, as My gift of love to you. There is no other victory. There is only striving after emptiness and wind. Blessed are you if you know this and remain faithful to it.

Do not chafe at the restrictions My cross lays upon you. Yield quickly to My way and let not your heart be troubled. I see all and know all—and I am with you every step of your way. *In this sign you will conquer.*

March Twelfth

He calleth his own sheep by name, and leadeth them out.

John 10:3

I call you by your name and you are Mine. From all eternity I have loved you and to eternity I shall love you. Your mind cannot comprehend this, but your heart can respond to it. Enough to know that you are known and loved.

What are all the baubles of this world in comparison with this? What is fame, power, riches?—things or conditions that pass away even as you use them. Embrace and hold fast this reality—this gift: you are known and loved.

March Thirteenth

According as He hath chosen us in Him before the foundation of the world, that we should be holy and without blame before Him in love.

Ephesians 1:4

In the course of your life, My hand has overshadowed you and protected you. My tender mercies have attended you and spared you. Do not ask why, or doubt that it is so. As you review the past, make it a sure foundation with which to face the future. The foundation is My overarching, unfailing love and care—a foundation that cannot fail.

March Fourteenth

For in Him we live and move, and have our being; as certain also of your own poets have said, For we are also His offspring.

Acts 17:28

You are nearer to Me than you know. I am nearer to you than you realize. Your sense of distance and separation are the fruit of your sin—your independence, pride, and self-absorption. These sins erect barriers in your soul, and they isolate you in a prison of your own making. Yet I am with you—nearer than you realize. Open the door in the wall you have built—or better still, begin anew the destruction of that barrier. It *can* be done—and My help is sure.

March Fifteenth

But the mercy of the Lord is from everlasting to everlasting upon them that fear Him.

Psalm 103:17

I am the Lord who healeth thee. The adversary meant evil to you, but I mean it for good and for life. Put aside the distractions that pull you from My chosen path. Take each day as a gift of love from the Giver of love. Purify your mind and thoughts with simple cries and prayers. Prove me by the waters of Meribah. Let me turn the bitter into sweet and trust that I can ever do so. None know this save those who choose to become "little children" before their heavenly Father. The oil of My mercy never runs out.

March Sixteenth

It is good for me that I have been afflicted; that I might learn Thy statutes.

Psalm 119:71

Frail, mortal child of flesh, My love is beyond your grasping. The mysteries of My providence often leave you trembling and confused. What you cannot understand with your mind, you fear. The darkness and shadows that must needs come fill you with uncertainty. Yet I tell you that in all the shadows there is light. In all the uncertainties there is one certainty—My eternal, unchanging love. See and find it. You cannot "grasp" it, but you are held by it.

March Seventeenth

The Lord hath done great things for us; whereof we are glad.

Psalm 126:3

Your prayer is heard, My child, your prayer is heard. The desire you express is not yours, but the gift of My Spirit. Flesh recoils at the prospect of its mortality. The spirit within yearns to be clothed with immortality. Cultivate the spirit within. Deny the flesh its grasping, clinging—its fearful demands to be pampered, loved, considered. Fight the battle in the strength I shall give and be whole-hearted in it. Call to mind, in the heat of battle, what great things I have done for you. I have taken your small, puny faith, and the steps you have taken in faith, and enlarged them beyond anything you can see. Only I know the extent of My blessing, but you can know enough to strengthen you and arm you when the adversary comes in like a flood. Play the man, My child. Your prayer is heard.

March Eighteenth

Hold fast the form of sound words, which thou hast heard of me, in faith and love which is in Christ Jesus.

II Timothy 1:13

Guard well, My child, the life I have given you. The adversary is ever seeking ways to nullify and make havoc of your faith. You are no match for him without Me, and you easily forget how dangerous it is to wander from the safe path. Let caution warn you not to be presumptuous. I am your safety, your front guard and your rear guard. You are safe when you stay with Me. That is how you guard the life I have given you.

March Nineteenth

Draw nigh to God, and He will draw nigh to you. Humble yourselves in the sight of the Lord, and He shall lift you up.

James 4:8,10

Call upon Me, and I will answer you. Draw near to Me, and I will draw near to you. This is ever My word and My promise. I know your frame and your weakness. I know the difficulty you have in staying your thoughts on Me. I know all about you—more, much more than you know about yourself. So come to Me in your brokenness, your failure to measure up, your craven, baseless fears. I will not turn you away, because I love you. You will come to know Me as I reveal My love to you. Call upon Me and I *will* answer you.

March Twentieth

Therefore with joy shall ye draw water out of the wells of salvation, and in that day shall ye say, Praise the Lord.

Isaiah 12:3,4

With joy you shall draw water from the wells of salvation. The wells are deep and sometimes you must wait for the plumbing of the depths. The surface of your soul is like the surface of the sea—busily moving in many directions at the gusts of wind that blow on it. There is a restlessness there that must be gotten past. Or change the picture, My child, and compare it to a dry and thirsty desert. Unstable and shifting in many directions. So do not be discouraged that I require you to go deeper than the shifting sand, the restless sea. Quietness is in the depths. The "water of salvation" is plentiful and pure, but must be drawn from its source. Since most of your life is lived on the surface, it is all the more necessary that you take the time to go deep and tap the life-giving wells.

March Twenty–first

For the Lord thy God is a merciful God. He will not forsake thee.
Deuteronomy 4:31

Fear not the path which I have laid out for you. Flinch not at what I ask you to bear. You will not bear it alone. Lo, I am with you, My child, in every moment. I tell you this because I know you from your conception in your mother's womb. She, too, feared many things. Your feeling of aloneness and abandonment are made more intense by your sin. The fear you feel is a punishment for your rebellion against My love. All rebellion is against My love, because I, the Lord, am love. That is the essence of My nature. You are a creature, a creation of My love. When you understand that simple truth, you will know freedom from fear. You will know that I will never leave you nor forsake you. Never. That is my promise.

March Twenty–second

Moses said, "We are journeying unto the place of which the Lord said, I will give it to you."

Numbers 10:29

Press on past the barriers you meet in your earthly pilgrimage toward Me. Your tendency is to linger and let them delay your progress. Life is not static. It was not meant to be. The past is gone, yet present in your memory and in consequences of past decisions. The future is not yet, but present in the consequences which will flow from decisions made now. Lingering at the barriers is but a cowardly indulgence of faithlessness. The barriers of guilt, of anger and resentment, of fear, of grief—what are these compared with that which I have set before you? Press on toward the Light. Again I say, press on!

March Twenty–third

Break up your fallow ground: for it is time to seek the Lord, till He come and rain righteousness upon you.

Hosea 10:12

Feast on My Word. This is the true food for your soul. The words that I speak to you, they are spirit and they are life. By this I mean that they become sustenance for your spirit and life for your soul. I quicken "words" by My Spirit so that they become expressions of My Word.

You need to trust, to learn to trust, the living word that comes to you. My word comes to break up the hard, fallow ground of your heart. Do you not see it? Is it not happening? But there is much work still to be done. I am the Restorer of breaches. I am He who breaks down walls of separation.

March Twenty–fourth

For thou hast possessed my reins: thou hast covered me in my mother's womb.

Psalm 139:13

My dear child, I accept your thanks and praise. I am glad for you that you recognize My great tenderness and compassion toward you all the days of your life. I saw you in your mother's womb and set you apart for My purposes. I watched you in your disobediences and in your guilt and pain. I am God and not man, that I should abandon My purpose. Yes, you caused Me pain in your hard-headed, self-chosen way. You have inflicted pain on others, too. The process of healing is still going on, and your faithful repentance must be part of that process. Keep the stream of gratitude flowing, for it gives life to the necessary repentance. My glory shall yet be revealed. That is My promise.

March Twenty–fifth

And the barrel of meal wasted not, neither did the cruse of oil fail, according to the word of the Lord.

I Kings 17:16

My goodness never fails. If My people would only trust me more, they would see the unending stream of mercy flowing like a mighty river, an unending supply. Your life is a testimony to the surprising ways I use to supply the needs of My children. From the day you gave your heart to me, the cruse of oil has never run dry. Through lean times and fat, you have never "wanted" for what you needed. I have fed you with the finest wheat.

Go over them in your mind and praise My faithfulness! Surprise yourself anew at the remembrance of My goodness. There is a pattern there that I want you to recognize. This, too, is a part of the blessing I give you—the joy and trust that such memories bring.

March Twenty–sixth

Being confident of this very thing, that He which hath begun a good work in you will perform it until the day of Jesus Christ.

Philippians 1:6

In the safety of My care you may rest your soul. No harm can reach you here where My power and protection prevail. With lustful eye, you have often looked beyond that safety, fantasizing how much better life would be apart from the narrowness of My way. You have robbed yourself of much peace that was available to you.

My work is still going on in your soul. Yes, it is "repair work," and therefore slow and painstaking. But it is *My* work, and it must be done according to My design, not yours. If My ways seem strange, recall often My tender mercies. Stand on solid ground, look up, believe, and you *will* see the glory of God.

March Twenty–seventh

Whatsoever ye do in word or deed, do all in the name of our Lord Jesus, giving thanks to God and the Father by Him.

Colossians 3:17

You cannot be faithful to Me, My child, unless you are grateful. Gratitude is like the rich soil out of which grows the fruit of faithfulness. As long as other motives are mixed in your obedience, the fruit will not be perfect. Pride of achievement, the desire for recognition or reward, competition and jealousy—all these add bitterness to the fruit. Gratitude is the theme of heaven's praise. It binds My people's hearts to Me and to one another, and destroys dividing walls. So do not lag in the exercise of this grace. Gratitude is the key that unlocks the inner treasury of grace.

March Twenty–eighth

*For godly sorrow worketh repentance to salvation not to be repented of;
but the sorrow of the world worketh death.*

II Corinthians 7:10

Can you see, My child, how the rod of My judgment is the rod
of My mercy? Can you agree with Me that the rod was a necessary
part of your healing and salvation? Bitterness spoils the fruit borne
of such judgment and mercy. I will cleanse it from you if you are
willing to let it go.

You are still too defensive before "verbal onslaughts." Your walls
of defense, your inner deafness to the essential truth being spoken are
very hurtful, and I want you to give them up. Your pride is a poor
substitute for the freedom I offer in its place. "Don't stint yourself!"

March Twenty–ninth

When I am weak, then I am strong.

II Corinthians 12:10

I have seen your affliction. The wounds and scars of your soul are
not hidden from Me. "I am the Lord that healeth thee." That is My
gracious and self–chosen work within you, My child. It is My work,
and yours to accept with faith and gratitude. Let no thoughts from
the adversary bring doubts in your mind about My purpose and My

power. I do not work as man works, and the process is largely hidden from your view. This is where I call on you to fight doubt and discouragement and to exercise faith in Me. I give you this part of the battle out of My love for you. Don't try to *understand*, but stand *under* the mercy which covers you.

March Thirtieth

I will pray with the spirit, and I will pray with the understanding also; I will sing with the spirit, and I will sing with the understanding also.
                                                                I Corinthians 14:15

Pray with your eyes open. Pray with your heart open. Pray with your ears open—open to Me and My word. Pray with a song in your heart, a song of deliverance, a song of thanksgiving. Fit yourself to be in My company with repentance and confession—covered with My forgiveness and the mantle of My mercy. Thus we can have sweet concourse together—a blessing to you and a joy to My fatherly heart. Put away fear of offending Me as long as you observe to do what I have told you. A lively, living trust is more pleasing than groveling at My feet. Enter My presence with thanksgiving, and come *boldly* to the Throne of grace. I welcome you, My beloved child.

March Thirty–first

Sow to yourselves in righteousness, reap in mercy; break up your fallow ground; for it is time to seek the Lord, till he come and rain righteousness upon you.

Hosea 10:12

Break up the fallow ground. Break up the hard tracks of your mind, hardened with the frequent footprints of your old thinking patterns. Tend the new plants of My planting, the engrafted Word, the living knowledge that I impart on a daily basis. Your life is meant to be *lived*, not endured. It is a gift, not a cursing. Recognize and welcome My comings, My appointments, My tender mercies. Break up the hardened tracks—and *live*.

APRIL

Holy Spirit, Truth divine,
  Dawn upon this soul of mine;
Word of God and inward light,
  Wake my spirit, clear my sight.

Holy Spirit, Love divine,
  Glow within this heart of mine;
Kindle every high desire;
  Perish self in Thy pure fire.

Samuel Longfellow
1819-1892

April First

All flesh is grass, and all the goodliness thereof is as the flower of the field. The grass withereth, the flower fadeth; but the word of our God shall stand forever.

Isaiah 40:6,8

All flesh is grass, and all the goodliness thereof as the flower of the grass. The flower withereth and the grass fadeth. But the Word of the Lord endureth—forever.

Before Me the generations rise and pass away. I call them to Myself. Eternity is little in your thoughts and plans. The immediate and near future occupy your mind. Yet I have called you, and do call you, to be with Me in eternity. Can you not see how that changes the perspective on *every* earthly circumstance and relationship? Oh, the blindness of My people! You scurry about and worry about these little, trivial, passing things—and neglect the one thing needful—preparing for your eternal destiny. I have given My Word—and it stands forever. Do not depart from it to the left nor to the right. Seek My face. Seek My blessing. Trust me in all the relationships of your life. They are in My keeping. Sickness, separation—and death—cannot destroy that which I keep safe. I know when to give and when to withhold. I am with you for good.

April Second

And walk in love, as Christ also hath loved us, and hath given himself for us an offering and a sacrifice to God.

Ephesians 5:2

Begin and end the day with Me, My child. Let the hours between be a walking together in love. Remember that you are My servant, and you are responsible to spend the hours in My service. Your life is not your own. You have been bought with a great price. Do not take it back to yourself, for that is robbery. Learn what it means to be a purchased possession—a ransomed soul. Live out your freedom in the light of who I am and who you are. Begin and end the day with Me, My child, and let all the hours between be a walking together in love.

April Third

O taste and see that the Lord is good.

Psalm 34:8

To taste, you must take the food into yourself. Taste is a way of trying, of testing the goodness of the food. In like manner, the tasting, the testing of spiritual food is a necessary part of your experience. You have "tasted" many unhealthy substitutes, and your soul was wounded—harmed—by taking in corrupting and tainted substances. The effects have been serious but not fatal, because My sovereign purpose over-ruled your foolish choices.

Taste and see the food that I supply—the nourishing and healing food of My Word and Spirit. Doubt not that I am the Bread of life—and that I stand the "taste test"!

April Fourth

Who maketh the clouds His chariot; who walketh upon the wings of the wind.

Psalm 104:3

Clouds and storms are also part of My way. The sunshine of My grace is hidden from view as they do their necessary work. See how in My natural world these things play their necessary role to the ongoing of life, and be aware, My child, of their beneficial role in your spiritual life. Clouds and storms are also part of My way.

April Fifth

Be not deceived; God is not mocked: for whatsoever a man soweth that shall he also reap.

Galatians 6:7

My loving kindness is ever before you. There is no end to it. What you perceive as judgment or wrath in no way contradicts it. I cannot be false to Myself—and I am not like you. My sternness is also an expression of My mercy.

April Sixth

But ye are come to Mount Zion, and unto the city of the living God, the heavenly Jerusalem, and to an innumerable company of angels.

Hebrews 12:22

"The place whereon you stand is holy ground." All ground is holy when it becomes a place of meeting. I am ever with you, and yet there need to be these places and times where My glory breaks through to you. You could not bear yet to live constantly in the vision of My glory. Your eyes and your heart are not yet prepared. But these glimpses are foretastes, and they are My gift to you.

April Seventh

Let your light so shine before men, that they may see your good works and glorify your Father which is in heaven.

Matthew 5:16

I am the Light of the world. In Me there is no darkness at all. My light still shines in the darkness of this world, and it will never be put out. You, My child, live in a mixture of light and darkness. Some of the darkness is your own choice, because you "love darkness rather than light." You fear too much light because your pride hides your secret thoughts and sins. Humble yourself before Me, and do not fear what any human may say or think. Light brings life. Darkness brings death. My will for you is LIFE.

April Eighth

But grow in grace, and in the knowledge of our Lord and Savior Jesus Christ. To Him be glory both now and for ever.

II Peter 3:18

Becoming. You are becoming that for which I created and redeemed you. You are becoming what you are not yet. You are becoming what only I can see. When your love for Me is perfected, there will be no fear of Me. When you know as you are known, there will be no need to hide. Where My image and My plan have become what you are, then fullness of joy will be yours. In the meantime, My child, press toward the mark. Keep becoming.

April Ninth

But he was wounded for our transgressions, he was bruised for our iniquities: the chastisements of our peace was upon Him; and with His stripes we are healed.

Isaiah 53:5

When I was crucified, I gave up My life for your sake and the sake of My other children. I did it in obedience to My Father and yours, and tasted the bitter uncertainties that you face in death. It was a real battle, and I want you to realize that you have the same weapons in your fight that I had in Mine. I have promised you My help in all your needs. I keep My promises. I am the Faithful One. Remember this.

April Tenth

For we are his workmanship, created in Christ Jesus unto good works, which God hath before ordained that we should walk in them.

Ephesians 2:10

My dear child, your identity as My child does not depend on you. You have been created, redeemed and called by My sovereign will, and your sonship rests on that solid foundation. Do not forget that you were bought with a great price, and allow that fact to hold you steady when temptations assault your soul. The adversary will attempt to sow doubts and distance in our relationship. Press closer to Me.

April Eleventh

For ye see your calling, brethren, how that not many wise men after the flesh, not many mighty, not many noble, are called: But God hath chosen the foolish things of the world to confound the wise.

I Corinthians 1:26,27

I have not called you to greatness as the world counts greatness. Yours is to be plowed under, the seed that falls into the ground that life may spring forth. My life in you requires a corresponding death in yours. This is done in part by the denial of your craving for recognition and applause.

The glory I offer you will not feed your sin-appetite. When I lead you "from glory to glory" you will know and recognize that the glory is Mine and the blessing of it is more than all the world could give.

April Twelfth

I say unto you, there is joy in the presence of the angels of God over one sinner that repenteth.

Luke 15:10

My dear child, put away vain thoughts and regrets. I know all your way—and I have never abandoned you, no matter how far you strayed from the straight path of My will. Let this be a cause of rejoicing and thanksgiving, even as you mourn the folly of your self-directed course. Repentance is forward-looking, not backward-gazing. I am God, and still restore the locust-eaten years. Your great need, My child, is more faith in Me.

April Thirteenth

But I say to you, Love your enemies, bless them that curse you, do good to them that hate you, and pray for them which despitefully use you and persecute you.

Matthew 5:44

Bless those who love you and those who hate you. That is My command and that is the path to healing. I have allowed some to respond negatively to your sin without the covering of My love. They reacted to what they saw and felt in you, without the covering of mercy. So their feelings are the *natural* outcome of soul meeting soul. On your part, because of the light I have given you, you must take responsibility for your sins and their reaction. Don't ask if that is fair! That is not the point. Do you want healing? Do you desire My will? Those are the questions, and if the answer is Yes, then the path will lead you to where you want to go. Watch out for the "demon of self-justification." Remember—when My mercy is removed, your sin, your nature *naturally* causes a negative reaction—hate. That should be ample material for ongoing repentance—and a deep desire to claim My mercy over all your relationships. And remember this word, My child: Blessed are the merciful, for *they* shall obtain mercy. You will always be in need of that.

April Fourteenth

O death, where is thy sting? O grave, where is thy victory? The sting of death is sin, and the strength of sin is the law. But thanks be to God, which giveth us the victory through our Lord Jesus Christ.

I Corinthians 15:55-57

O My child, hear My good word to you today. Death has been defeated. It no longer has dominion over my people. I am the Lord, and I choose how to call each of My own to Me. Death is a door—a door out and a door in. For My children, a door out of suffering and pain, with all the uncertainties they feel in this earthly life; a door into the life I have prepared for you. That is enough for you—if you will remain close to Me. You do not need to know more, just that through that door, I will be waiting for you.

April Fifteenth

But whoso hath this world's goods, and seeth his brother have need, and shutteth up his bowels of compassion from him, how dwelleth the love of God in him?

I John 3:17

This is my word today: compassion. Pray for compassion! You have an unmerciful heart. You rejoice at the discomfiture of those who have offended you. You place yourself "above" them in your mind, forgetting who and what you are in truth. Your harsh and unmerciful attitude puts a wall—a strong barrier between us. Little wonder that you are then plagued with fear and anxiety. I am your peace; I am the place of tranquility and quietness—but an unmerciful heart cannot dwell there.

April Sixteenth

Where wast thou when I laid the foundations of the earth? When the morning stars sang together and all the sons of God shouted for joy?

Job 38:4,7

The day is Mine. It is a gift of My love to My creation. The sun shines at My behest, and light goes forth according to My will. My creation does not understand, and takes it all for granted. But a few souls can see and know. Be one of them, My child, and enter into the secret joy of thankfulness. Take *nothing* for granted any more. Praise and gratitude carry their own reward. You cannot become what I created you to be by any other path.

April Seventeenth

There failed not ought of any good thing which the Lord had spoken to Israel; all came to pass.

Joshua 21:45

My child, do not doubt My love. Put away the accusing thoughts that rise in your mind. These are not from Me, but from the enemy camp. Rehearse often the footprints of My deliverances and My provision. Trace the outlines of My mercy.

The supply of manna never ran short for My people. It has never run short for you. There have always been the angels of My presence to aid and provide what you needed. The more you realize this, the more your gratitude will displace your doubts.

April Eighteenth

I will put upon you no other burden, but hold fast that which ye have already till I come.

Revelation 2:24,25

The burden of My word is a light burden. It must be borne faithfully, My child. Carry it in your heart throughout the day, a companion to your thoughts and actions. Carry it as a treasure, more precious than gold, for it is that. "The love of Jesus, what it is, None but His loved ones know." That word is appropriate here.

April Nineteenth

Today if ye will hear his voice, harden not your hearts, as in the provocation.

Hebrews 3:15

Today, if you hear My voice, do not harden your heart. Keep open to My leading and My wisdom. Let My word dwell in you, and its fruit will bring blessing to others. You will be able to see and rejoice.

Hardening your heart is closing yourself in to your own reasoning and wisdom. They bear no fruit and bring no life, even though they may make a show of themselves. Be on guard against this tendency in you, because I am offering you another way.

April Twentieth

Thus saith the Lord: Again there shall be heard in this place the voice of joy, and the voice of gladness, the voice of them that shall say, Praise the Lord of hosts: for the Lord is good; for his mercy endureth for ever; and of them that shall bring the sacrifice of praise into the house of the Lord.
Jeremiah 33:10,11

In this I am well pleased—that you offer Me your heartfelt praise. You have nothing else to give but your love and obedience to My holy will. I know how imperfect and stumbling your obedience is. I know your continual need of forgiveness and cleansing. But I also know your heart, and I am at work in healing the breaches, driving out the darkness that still lurks within. As you offer heartfelt praise to Me, you open yourself more fully to My saving work within. In this I am well pleased.

April Twenty–first

And therefore will the Lord wait, that he may be gracious unto you, and therefore will he be exalted, that he may have mercy on you.

Isaiah 30:18

My dear child, this truly is the throne of grace. It is purely My grace alone that makes these meetings possible. You have neither earned nor deserved the privilege I have given you. Magnify My grace in your heart. Put down any feelings or thoughts that you are "special." It is enough that I love you, include you in the circle of My little ones, have pity on you and convey My truth to your soul. That is reason enough for an eternity of gratitude on your part.

April Twenty–second

In my Father's house are many mansions: if it were not so, I would have told you. I go to prepare a place for you.

John 14:2

I have heard your cry and I know the longing of your heart. It was I who put the longing for home within you. Without that, you would have become a spiritual wanderer, a truly "homeless" person.

Do not grow weary in the time of waiting. Do not let yourself be confused or confounded by what seem to be unexplained delays. Trust can only grow amid uncertainties. Trust is the strong bond that holds during all storms and crises. Faith lays hold on the promise; trust *keeps* hold through all the trials. Waiting is part of your training in trust.

April Twenty–third

There shall no evil befall thee, neither shall any plague come nigh thy dwelling.

Psalm 91:10

"A thousand shall fall at your side, and ten thousand at your right hand, but it shall not come near you." Because each child of Mine is My peculiar and particular care, this saying is true. My protection is over you, to keep you in all your ways. This is not an excuse for presumption or pride, but for humble gratitude.

Make the best of the days I have given you to live. Do not waste them in idleness or despair. Play the man! Gird yourself for battle against the enemy's assaults—and honor Me in your victories.

April Twenty–fourth

The peace of God which passeth all understanding shall keep your hearts and minds through Christ Jesus.

Philippians 4:7

The peace that passes understanding is an active power, an active stillness that stirs hope and joy even in the midst of trouble. As long as you are in the world there will be trouble, tribulation, trials. These are not to destroy you nor to dampen your faith in Me, but to purify your soul and wean it from its captivity to a passing world. Not yet has it become firmly attached to that which cannot be shaken, so with every blow to its false security a choice is open to choose the better part.

I know your fears—from your own weakness and of what might lie ahead for you. I call you now to trust yourself to My care, to lean on My strength, to rest on My promise. Your fears will subside, they are not omnipotent—I am. They are subject to Me and to your obedience to Me. As your love for Me grows, they will diminish. Peace replaces panic. I, the Lord, reign.

April Twenty–fifth

Wait on the Lord. Be of good courage, and He shall strengthen thine heart. Wait, I say, on the Lord.

Psalm 27:14

Waiting is a purifying time. The desires of your heart must line up with My desires, or I would be guilty of aiding you in sin. My desire for you is entirely in keeping with My character—and to the end that I have in mind for you. That end is love and the whole length of the journey toward that end is filled with My love for you. Therefore, My child, wait. Be of good courage, and in very truth I will give you your heart's desires.

April Twenty–sixth

My soul fainteth for Thy salvation; but I hope in Thy word.

Psalm 119:81

My child, do not despair that My plans are taking a long time to work out. You cannot see the future nor the pitfalls along the way. These delays are given to purify your heart and the hearts of others, that you and they will be ready for the healing My power will effect. What is required of you now is to continue to purge all the old leaven of bitterness and unforgiveness. That purging goes deep and produces many tears of repentance if it is to be complete. The Kingdom of heaven is still "at hand" for those who repent. My Kingdom comes whenever and wherever true repentance opens the door. Since I dwell within the "broken and contrite heart," it is not necessary to wait for some future event to see the Kingdom. You will know—and see—that I am God. My glory can be seen in small as well as great things.

April Twenty–seventh

A bruised reed shall He not break, and the smoking flax shall He not quench.

Isaiah 42:3

Yes, I am your Lord and your God. It is I who give you life and breath moment by moment. You are entirely in My care. I touch not only the mountain but hearts, setting them aflame with My love.

Nourish the flame, My child. Vain regret is not repentance. Keep open to the breath of My Spirit and open to My love. Obey the gentle commands and become more sensitive to My ways. Be strong and of good courage, and I will strengthen your heart. I am able to do exceedingly beyond all your poor mind can ask or think.

April Twenty–eighth

Call upon me in the day of trouble; I will deliver thee, and thou shalt glorify me.

Psalm 50:15

Call upon me, My child, and I will answer you. Not only do My sheep hear My voice, but I hear the voice of My sheep. Marvel not that among the millions of voices on earth, I hear and recognize the voices of My own. You think this is presumptuous—to count yourself among "My own." It is only that you are realizing in greater depth and intensity what it means to be claimed by My love. Leave the mysteries to Me, child. Quiet your soul as a little child. My Presence now can quiet every fear.

Let your situation work My purpose out in your inner life, and it will bring forth fruit in your works. First things first.

April Twenty–ninth

Our God shall come and shall not keep silence. Hear, O my people, and I will speak.

Psalm 50:3,7

As you listen for My voice, I listen for your prayers. I created you to have this fellowship with Me. Yes, it is a foretaste—a small beginning of what I have prepared for My children. But it is only that—a small beginning. As you have been listening during these past weeks, you have come to a greater longing for My living word to you. I know that, and I am faithful. I mean to touch and continue to touch your heart and spirit at a very deep level—beyond your rational understanding. There, in the hidden depth, a fresh work is being done—breaking and preparing for that which is still to come.

Be content to know that I love you and hear your cry. Rejoice in every place and circumstance where you recognize My hand. I am here—for you. Do not be downcast at those who are against you. It will all work out for good. That is my solemn promise.

April Thirtieth

Thou shalt put the mercy seat above upon the ark. . . . and there I will meet with thee and commune with thee from above the mercy seat.
                                                                    Exodus 25:21,22

My dear child, comfort your heart at My mercy seat. Here there is a foretaste of the blessedness which I have prepared for you and all My children. Here there is a breakthrough from the dullness and opaqueness that characterizes most of your life. That is the well-spring of your tears—the unguardedness of your heart. Do not be surprised that no great "words" or revelations come in these meetings. You do not need them. What you need, child, is the assurance of My love and care. I see you trying to reach out and make "connections" in different directions—children, family, friends—and for the most part they fail you. But that is because they cannot supply what only I can give. Remember the word, "Thou openest Thy hand and satisfieth the desire of every living thing." One thing must precede that: the shaping of the desire away from destructive ends. When the heart is at peace, yearning for that which is withheld ceases. All things are yours when your heart is at peace.

So come to this seat often—this mercy seat. I have promised in My holy Word: I will meet with you here. Learn here the secret of My love.

MAY

O let me hear Thee speaking
   In accents clear and still,
Above the storm of passion,
   The murmurs of self-will;
O speak to reassure me,
   To hasten or control;
O speak, and make me listen,
   Thou Guardian of my soul.

John E. Bode
1816-1874

May First

Happy is the man that findeth wisdom, and the man that getteth under-standing. Her ways are ways of pleasantness, and all her paths are peace.
Proverbs 3:13,17

Walk in My ways today, My child. My ways are ways of blessed-ness and peace. Mine is a safe way—surrounded by all the protection you need from the enemy.

Leave to me the concerns about the future—your future and that of those you love. The future is in My hands, and you can safely entrust it to Me.

Redeem the time. The days are short and much has been wasted in your past years. But it is enough—and I will be with you to claim the present for My purposes. Be of good cheer!

May Second

And now, Lord, what do I wait for? My hope is in Thee.
Psalm 39:7

Hope! Hope! Hope! Hope is My gift in the interim time—when your heart is turned toward Me. There is no place for hopelessness in your relationship with Me, for the future—your future—is in My hand. Your sins of worry and fear are like acids that eat away at the hope I give you. Hope is like a beckoning light before you, and is meant to encourage you when things are difficult. It is a precious gift. Do not waste it!

My sovereign will none can thwart. That is why hope is a trustworthy guide. You do not need to understand all mysteries, how I shall accomplish My will—either in you or in others. But you do need to claim and cherish and *nourish* the gift of Hope.

Bid others be of good cheer. Too much fear darkens the hearts of My people. Bid them be of good cheer! The darkness cannot prevail because the true Light has come. Become a people of praise.

May Third

Thus saith the Lord God, the Holy One of Israel; in returning and rest shall ye be saved; in quietness and in confidence shall be your strength.
Isaiah 30:15

Quietness is difficult for you because you have yet to learn to direct your thoughts and "stay" them on Me. You love the wanderings of your mind and easily let them carry you away.

Stillness is a state of rest in My presence. It is My gift to you when you are ready for it. Much of the turmoil you experience is the fruit of your own choices and the consequences of your wandering mind. Instead of wandering, My child, try *wondering*.

May Fourth

He hath made everything beautiful in its time.

Ecclesiastes 3:11

The beauty of this world does not compare with the glory of the next. It is, however, a foretaste, just as the peace I give here is a foretaste of My Kingdom. Enjoy the beauty here. It is my gift to you. I put the hunger for it in your heart, and it is I who fulfill that hunger.

Embrace the life to which I have called you. Do not question My purposes, for they are hidden from you for your good. Your walk will have many thorns—but always there will be beauty—and the thorns are protective against that which would destroy. O My child, let the beauty of My world open your eyes more eagerly to the beauty of My life, My Kingdom. You have only begun to touch the hem of My garment, the edges of My ways.

May Fifth

We . . . have fled for refuge to lay hold upon the hope set before us: which hope we have as an anchor of the soul, both sure and steadfast.

Hebrews 6:18,19

Cling to My cross. It is the anchor of your soul. Wild thoughts, ideas, temptations—all would dash you to pieces. Here, only here, is your safety. It is the Rock of Ages—and in it there is safety through every storm.

Cling to My cross. For there you know of very surety that your only claim on Me is My sovereign love. You did not create it—it was before you. You do not control it or destroy it—for I am God. But clinging here, you can keep a fresh awareness of the relationship between us. It is based not on merit but on grace.

You are a very insecure soul—never fully trusting for more than a moment. Your faith is still weak and puny—and far from the robust health I will for it. Your past trials have had some results—but O, My child, how much more you could have learned from My goodness!

May Sixth

Behold, I will do a new thing; now it shall spring forth; shall ye not know it?

Isaiah 43:19

My dear child, I am writing a new word upon your heart. Heretofore you have never fully accepted My love in its simplicity. Anxiety and fear have shut the door against My proffered presence. Sin and rebellion within, then, have wreaked havoc in the place where I would have reigned. Confusion and misdirection prevailed where order and progress could have been manifest. You know in part some of the pain and distress that resulted.

You weep now. Others have wept for you—and prayed that your eyes might be open to the truth. Do not close your heart to Me. Do not let pride shut out my abiding, guiding presence. I am here to bless you, and through you to bless others. At eventide there shall be light.

May Seventh

I would that ye should understand that the things which happened unto me have fallen out rather unto the furtherance of the gospel.
Philippians 1:12

Your disappointments of the past were but steps along the path that led you back to Me. Know that no good thing do I withhold from them that love Me. But when your desires and ambitions led you in contrary ways, I wisely cut them off to safe limits—having always in view that which would *ultimately* satisfy your deepest desire. That is My wisdom and mercy—it is always in operation, unseen and unrecognized by My children. So your disappointments become inconsequential—*except* that they are signal points of My overruling hand of mercy on you. Believe this, My child, and count it all joy. There is not loss—no ultimate loss—to you if you will accept My higher gift—the treasure of My love in the secret place of your heart. So few find it! Be one of them.

May Eighth

Behold, what manner of love the Father hath bestowed upon us, that we should be called the sons of God.

I John 3:1

I honor those who honor Me. My honor is not like the world's honor. When I honor a soul, it is by drawing such a one close to My side. This may be the call to suffer "dishonor" in the world's eye. It may be a place of total or near-total obscurity. But the soul can know—indeed must come to know—that a signal honor has been bestowed. None call on Me in vain. My mercy is not meager, not in short supply. Don't be surprised by My goodness and generosity. *Expect* it. Pray that your heart will also become enlarged with mercy.

May Ninth

He healeth the broken in heart, and bindeth up their wounds.

Psalm 147:3

I am the Lord who healeth thee. My Spirit goes forth to renew the souls of My people—souls that are wounded and torn by the thorns of this fallen world. They are thorns of worldly care and fleshly lust, of ambition and pride, stubbornness and hardness of heart. All together they form a kind of obstacle course over which you must go to complete your journey. Left unhealed these wounds prove fatal. Their infection spreads to others as well. My healing has a double effect. It binds up and purifies the soul and intervenes between souls.

Much of My healing is hidden from view, even to the soul itself. So do not doubt the process. It *is* going on. I am the Lord who healeth *thee*.

May Tenth

Be careful for nothing; but in every thing by prayer and supplication with thanksgiving let your requests be made known unto God. And the peace of God which passeth all understanding, shall keep your hearts and minds through Christ Jesus.

Philippians 4:6,7

Peace be with you, My child. A settled peace is My gift to you, if you will accept it. In your earthly pilgrimage you have known little inward peace. You have not been at peace with yourself or your circumstances. A constant restlessness stirred within. When you caught a glimpse of heavenly peace, it was from a far country.

I give My peace to those who will receive it. It is a pearl of great price, but it cannot abide in a heart bent on its own way. My will is peace, and in spite of difficulties brings peace to the heart. Peace be with you, My child.

May Eleventh

They that sow in tears shall reap in joy.

Psalm 126:5

Tears are never wasted. Tears and prayers belong together, for real prayer comes from the depths of your heart. Both joy and sorrow flow from the fount of tears. They are My gift to you, washing away the soil of many years, softening the hardness which has long encrusted your heart. Do not be ashamed of them nor frightened by their arrival. Wholeness demands a cleansing and a plowing up of fallow ground. Abundant fruit can come forth only from hearts that are softened and made workable. Keep at it, My child, and *expect* harvest to come.

May Twelfth

That I may know Him, and the power of his resurrection, and the fellowship of his sufferings, being made conformable unto his death.

Philippians 3:10

Avoiding suffering is avoiding Me, for I am there for you. I do not delight in seeing My children in pain. I do not willingly afflict the children of men. But you know, My child, that I have suffered for you, and that those who love Me are given to share in My sufferings. You do not, you cannot, understand this with your natural mind. Only the experience itself can reveal what I am saying.

You have not been a willing participant in My suffering, and have sought various ways to avoid it. Only My persistent love that would not let you go prevailed—and you see a little clearer, do you not, the secrets hidden there? There is no cause for fear—only faithful assent to that which I allow. It will be all right.

May Thirteenth

Wherefore seeing we also are compassed about with so great a cloud of witnesses, let us lay aside every weight, and the sin which doth so easily beset us, and let us run with patience the race that is set before us, looking unto Jesus, the author and finisher of our faith.

Hebrews 12:1,2

The mystery of the communion of saints is the mystery of prayer. It is the opening up of the barrier that now separates those who are earth-bound and those who have "made it home." Remembering those who have gone ahead is part of this communion. Keeping the memory alive—even generations removed—is an important part. You are all bound together in My love, and you are called to be a praying people. I allow for many mistakes in your struggle to understand, for I know how limited your capacities are. But I want you to keep seeking, knocking and asking, that your capacity may grow, and that you participate more freely in this blessed communion.

May Fourteenth

He shall feed his flock like a shepherd: he shall gather the lambs with his arm, and carry them in his bosom, and shall gently lead those that are with young.

Isaiah 40:11

This is the life I have given you. Embrace it and be grateful for it. I am the Good Shepherd who leads My sheep in the right places for *them*. Here, My design is to keep you in a safe place. Here those qualities I desire to see can come forth and grow if you will embrace this life. Worry not about what others may think. Instead, concern yourself about what *I* think.

May Fifteenth

Blessed be the God and Father of our Lord Jesus Christ, who hath blessed us with all spiritual blessings in heavenly places in Christ.

Ephesians 1:3

I bless you, My child, because you are Mine. Not because of your merits or achievements—for you know they are not worthy of My blessing. No, but because My favor rests on you and I have chosen to make you one of Mine, the blessing comes.

You are worried and anxious about many small things. They pass into eternity in a moment. You fear what might lie ahead for you—but do you doubt My blessing? Away with your infantile pre-occupations! The hour is late. Enter into the *blessing* I am giving you *today*. Harden not your heart against Me in fear.

May Sixteenth

For God hath not given us the spirit of fear; but of power, and of love, and of a sound mind.

II Timothy 1:7

The enemies are within, My child. Over the years you have given room for hiding places for them. They are permitted to plague you until your repentance is complete. Complete repentance means a final and absolute turning from the sin-filled fantasies and thoughts you have indulged. A holy hatred of the Babylonish garment is required.

As long as the harassing fears and foreboding come, fight against them with the weapons I have provided—believing prayer and grateful praise. They cannot prevail against these, and their attacks will turn to blessing.

May Seventeenth

But blessed are your eyes, for they see; and your ears, for they hear.
Matthew 13:16

Behold, behold, behold! You have eyes to see, but how often you miss seeing My blessing and My hand at work! Blindness still covers your sight, because you do not look *into* and *beyond* the surface of the things around you. I am offering you in these latter days a new depth of insight into the realities around you. You have preferred the surface-look because it did not disturb your fixed and "rational" ways of thinking. But I call you to a more mature and realistic walk in these days. Behold. Look deeper. Don't be put off by surface answers and explanations. I am at work in *every* situation for good. And you are to announce that over and over again—for your sake and for the sake of others. Be faithful.

May Eighteenth

Thus saith the Lord, Stand ye in the ways, and see, and ask for the old paths, where is the good way, and walk therein, and ye shall find rest for your souls.

Jeremiah 6:16

You are walking a new path—and yet an old path. It was offered you long ago, but you were not ready to receive it. In these intervening years you have wandered far from that path—sometimes very near the pit of destruction. Only My grace and Fatherly hand kept you back. The many crooks and turns in your pilgrimage were the results of these two forces—your blindness and My grace. Remember, My child, that I am afflicted in the affliction of My children, and I do not willingly cause grief to those I love. Yet I use the grief and the affliction for My purposes. But it is My will that you walk this path. Fear not. It is a good path and I am your protection in it. Have I not proven that through these long years? I will bless you and make you a blessing. Leave that to Me. That is My promise.

May Nineteenth

To appoint unto them that mourn in Zion, to give unto them beauty for ashes, the oil of joy for mourning, the garment of praise for the spirit of heaviness.

Isaiah 61:3

I come to you laden with gifts, gifts of My love. I am the Divine Giver, and it is My pleasure to bestow upon My children the gift of My love. There is the gift of understanding and light—as the light of My truth penetrates the darkness of your doubt and fearful hesitation. There is the gift of faith that enables you to receive and write these words. And, of course, My child, the gift of compunction and repentance, for you still have great need of them.

My hand is open toward those who love Me, and My ear is open to their cry. Fear not! Your prayer is heard—and the answer is prepared ahead of time. You are still too inexperienced and untrustworthy to be told more than this. Sometimes My gift is the patience to wait. In the meantime, you can praise My faithfulness.

May Twentieth

I exhort therefore, that, first of all, supplications, prayers, intercessions, and giving of thanks be made for all men.

I Timothy 2:1

Pray, pray, pray that My holy will shall come to pass. You do not know how important your faithfulness in prayer is to the accomplishment of My will. I have so honored My creation as to limit My own power to make room for a praying people. You have not understood this, nor the honored privilege I have bestowed on you in regard to prayer. A little light has begun to dawn in the thicket of opinion. That thicket has stood between you and the vast opportunity I offer you in prevailing prayer. My dear child, set aside your reasoning, and bring your deep cares, anxieties, and petitions to Me. I invite you to *prevail* with Me, for this is the doorway to a deeper level of trust, a new level of understanding of our relationship. Please do not fear to pray *bold* prayers, and *keep* praying when things look grim.

May Twenty–first

With everlasting kindness will I have mercy on thee, saith the Lord thy Redeemer.

Isaiah 54:8

My child, My child, know this about Me. My love is unchangeable. It knows no waxing or waning. Your emotions are unstable—they wax warm and cold. But you are held in My unchanging love—even when you cannot feel it or recognize it. I have told you before that I am the Light in the midst of darkness—for in Me there is no shadow of turning. So when your way is dark, turn to Me as once you did to your earthly father. All is well, and secure, and *light* in My presence.

Go forth today in the joy of My victory. Remember, there are no small victories in the Kingdom. Every defeat of the enemy is important in your spiritual journey.

And remember this, My child: My love is unchangeable. Let your love grow toward Me and My perfect will.

May Twenty–second

Yet they tempted and provoked the most high God, and kept not His testimonies.

Psalm 78:56

Consider, My child, how often you have provoked Me, and how often I have forgiven you. Consider how bitter is the fruit of your nature. Do you wonder at the alienation of others? Consider, My child, how often you have tried My patience and sown discord into your life and the lives of others.

Let the pain of these memories help you make better choices—against your own discordant self. Seek peace and pursue it—with yourself and with those around you.

May Twenty–third

. . . a broken and a contrite heart, O God, thou wilt not despise.

Psalm 51:17 (RSV)

Once I spoke to Moses out of the burning bush. Now I speak to My people out of burning hearts. This means that there needs to be an ardent desire to hear My word before you can receive it. "He will fulfill the desire of them that fear Him." This is the condition for truly hearing My voice.

My word breaks your heart again and again. It breaks down strongholds and vain imaginations, to enable you to walk with Me in My paths, My chosen paths. Put aside your fears, open yourself to My love and goodwill, and walk with Me today. Rejoice and be glad for all I have done for you, My child. Do not be afraid to *love* Me with all your heart. I will not reject your love, imperfect though it is.

May Twenty–fourth

And grieve not the Holy Spirit of God, whereby ye are sealed unto the day of redemption.

Ephesians 4:30

Many, many times My Spirit is grieved at the waywardness of your mind. How easily you are distracted from My goals and My aims for you, in pursuit of your own. Your heart so often is hardened against the gentle leading of the Spirit—and He grieves over you as a mother over a wayward and disobedient child. There is no peace—no heart peace—for you in that condition. Inner stress and tension are its fruits.

There is a better way. Where you begin to feel this stress, turn and apologize—yes, I said "apologize"—to your Divine Companion for your rudeness and self-centeredness,—and ask Him to reveal to you the place or places where you have ignored and refused His help. He is your Helper and Defender. He *knows* the way—you do not. Listen to Him, for He is given to My children to lead them in the right path—home.

May Twenty–fifth

How lovely is Thy dwelling place, O Lord of hosts! Blessed are they that dwell in Thy house; ever singing Thy praise.

Psalm 84:1,4 (RSV)

Beautiful for habitation is My dwelling place. Beautiful the peace which I have given. Why then, My child, do you not choose to dwell with Me in that beauty? Why turn aside so quickly to the "delights" of the world—a fascination with things that pass away and leave only dust and ashes? The time is here for you to heed more faithfully the gentle nudge and guidance of My Spirit when your mind is distracted and drawn to these worldly concerns. The break in fellowship with Me is serious, and leaves you in greater danger than you realize. I have called you to a closer walk with Me, and this cannot become a reality until and unless you choose to fight—to *recognize* and resist the assault of the enemy of your soul. Do not exchange your birthright for a mess of pottage—mental junk!

May Twenty–sixth

And walk in love, as Christ also hath loved us, and hath given Himself for us an offering and a sacrifice to God for a sweetsmelling savor.
Ephesians 5:2

Walk in love as I have loved you. The hate and resentments that still remain in you stain and poison your soul, so that it cannot manifest My nature as I would have it do. I call you to continue this process of repentance and relinquishment—giving up your "right' to feeling justified in these corrosive and negative emotions. I want you to be *free* of them before you leave this earthly life. I will continue to lead and help you in this process, and you will know that this darkness is being cleansed. The enemy will attempt to discourage you and convince you that it cannot be done. But I tell you most solemnly, it can and *shall* be done if you will persevere. My love is greater than your sin. Walk in it.

May Twenty–seventh

There were they in great fear, where no fear was.

Psalm 53:5

I see in My people too much craven fear—which is but another form of self-love. They seek signs and wonders, and miss the real wonders that are taking place before their eyes. This is the blindness of heart which looks and sees not.

There is enough ground for fear in everyone that it is easily exploited by the enemy for his purposes—but he must have the ground of self-love before he can effect his work. I call My people to move forward into a future known to Me alone. I repeat—a future known to Me alone. Do not try to discern it before its time. Sufficient for today are My blessings and My promises.

May Twenty–eighth

They have healed also the hurt of my people slightly, saying "Peace, peace"; where there is no peace.

Jeremiah 6:14

Pray for My will in every situation—even when you feel that the enemy is prevailing, and your heart cries out in grief and pain. This is where the battle becomes fiercest, and the foe looks for any agreement you may make with him against My goodness. O child, be strong in this battle with the strength I supply. My will can never be evil; it can only be good.

As I manifest My glory in each victory, so I allow you to taste the fruit of that victory when you engage faithfully in battle. The greatest temptation is to give up, to resign from the field of conflict and seek false peace. If you do that, the enemy will pursue you, and you will not be prepared to win. Keeping your heart in line with My yet-unrevealed will, the enemy cannot assail that inner stronghold. He may rage furiously, but there we dwell together—the citadel of true faith.

May Twenty–ninth

Lord, Thou wilt ordain peace for us: for Thou also hast wrought all our works in us.

Isaiah 26:12

In My Spirit there is peace. In My Presence there is joy unspeakable and full of glory. My throne-room is filled with praise. It is My pleasure to see My children rejoicing in Me. This is why, when you enter the secret place of prayer and praise, your heart is touched deeply with this hidden joy. It is a foretaste of that which awaits the faithful soul, and is meant as a bulwark against the evil that assails you in this world.

There is another world—a world which you know now by faith. You are not yet ready for that world, but these glimpses are My gifts to you, that you may abide in My love and fight the good fight to the end. Be at peace, My child. In My spirit there is peace.

May Thirtieth

I am Alpha and Omega, the beginning and the ending, saith the Lord, which is, and which was, and which is to come, the Almighty.

Revelation 1:8

I am the beginning and source of your faith. I am the Fount from which flow the streams of life. I am the Truth that banishes the darkness of imagination and delusion. I am the End and Perfection of all your journey. Not only the Beginning and Ending, My child, but the Way between. It is only in Me that you will walk the homeward path. By staying *with* Me, living *in* Me, you can finish your course with joy. That is My desire for you—that you finish your course with joy.

May Thirty–first

By faith . . . he endured as seeing Him who is invisible.

Hebrews 11:27

Behold and see. Yes, how often have I called you in this way—to awaken your sluggish heart, to see beyond the natural sight of your eyes. "Seeing the invisible." But you have resisted the call, because it threatens the easy, surface look you have preferred. This is a handicap in your spiritual growth, a form of spiritual blindness.

You do not need to fear looking into the depths of your own soul. *Your sins are forgiven.* I remember them no more against you! You need only to see them to remember the pit from which you have been rescued, and the nature into which you lapse if you depart from Me. But I do not call you to a fearful walk. "My yoke is easy and My burden is light." I seek maturity and trust—growing trust—in your relationship with Me. Look beyond—see the invisible realities that I have placed in your view.

JUNE

Open my ears that I may hear
   Voices of truth Thou sendest clear;
And while the wave-notes fall on my ear,
   Everything false will disappear;
Silently now I wait for Thee,
   Ready, my God, Thy will to see.
Open my ears, illumine me,
   Spirit divine.

Clara H. Fiske Scott
1841-1897

June First

But to him that worketh not, but believeth on Him that justifieth the ungodly, his faith is counted for righteousness.

Romans 4:5

I am your righteousness—the only righteousness that will ultimately count. *Your* righteousness is always sullied and mixed with unworthy motives. This I accept and cleanse, because of My own mercy.

I call you to rejoice in My righteousness. It is peace and joy. There is no striving or strain in it. It *is*. I know your frame, that it is dust. But I have not despised the work of My hands. I have not turned My back on My redemption. You are part of a redeemed people, and you have been purchased at a great price, because I have set My love on you. Don't try to figure it out. You cannot. Let it humble you in the right way. Let it free you in the right way. Let it lift you up in the right way. Learn to *flow* in My Spirit—casting aside the weights and sins—even the *pride* in your "righteousness." My yoke is still easy and My burden is still light. Ponder what this means.

June Second

Have I been so long a time with you, and yet hast thou not known Me?
John 14:9

Little faith is better than no faith. Little faith in Me is better than great faith in yourself. I do not despise your little faith, but I do mean for it to grow. You have been in this way too long to be content with such a small and shriveled faith. I deserve better! I have not asked you for great human strength and courage. I know your frame and your fearful nature. But I have given you plenty of "faith material" with which to grow a robust faith. Where is the harvest, My child? Where?

June Third

For he knoweth our frame; he remembereth that we are dust.
Psalm 103:14

"Dust thou art and to dust shalt thou return" was spoken only of the physical flesh—the grain of wheat that must fall into the ground. The physical world is passing away and is destined to decay. But My kingdom, My realm is of another kind. Your glimpses of it are meant to reassure you and yes, *lure* you away from this passing-away world. Cling not to the world, My child. Let it fall away in My providential plan, and reach forth to grasp the eternal that will never fail. There is no sorrow in the loss if your heart sees and seeks the better part.

June Fourth

But when he saw the wind boisterous, he was afraid; and beginning to sink, he cried, saying, "Lord, save me." And immediately Jesus stretched forth His hand, and caught him.

Matthew 14:30,31

Come nearer to me, My child, and do not be afraid. As I reached out to Peter when his faith failed and he began to sink in the boisterous sea, so I am reaching out to you. You do not have to fear Me—for My love is greater than your sin.

You still put too much "stock" in what others think of you. Their good or bad opinions mean too much to you. So you take too much delight in the one, and suffer too much pain in the other. I am your Shield and great Reward. I am the Lord who forgives and redeems you. I am He whose love is unchangeable—and I offer you a fellowship deeper and more stable than you have ever known. I can be the crowning experience of your life—if you will come nearer to Me, and not be afraid of Me.

June Fifth

Heal me, O Lord, and I shall be healed; . . . for Thou art my praise.
Jeremiah 17:14

Praise My goodness, My child, in all things. The pain which I allow in your life, as well as the pleasure, is filled with My goodness. By praising My goodness, you extract the sweetness known only to those who love Me.

I have called you to be an instrument of praise. Most of My world is still full of bitterness and complaint. My goodness is ignored or rationalized, and people pass away without claiming the hidden blessing. I call forth instruments of praise. These are souls who can hear and *begin* to recognize the truth—a truth so magnificent, so full of grace, that people find it hard to believe.

Praise opens the heart to receive the truth of My goodness. It is not by reasoning, argument or logic—but by *praise* that this truth will build the temple for My dwelling in your heart. Praise My goodness, My child, in all things.

June Sixth

But I say unto you, Love your enemies, bless them that curse you, do good to them that hate you, and pray for them which despitefully use you and persecute you.

Matthew 5:44

Doubt not that My hand is here. Let no clouds sully the purpose for which I have brought you here. Many souls have been wounded—not yours alone. My mercy and grace are wider than you can know or imagine. The healing streams from My heart will pour forth for those who will receive them. You do not have to worry about that. Only do not doubt—do not delay to be open to what I am doing. Do not miss the blessing I have prepared for you. Remember, my child, these words of Mine: "Pray for those who hate you and for those who despitefully use you." That prayer will protect you from many assaults of your adversary.

June Seventh

I pray for them. I pray not for the world, but for them which Thou hast given Me; for they are thine. And all Mine are Thine, and Thine are Mine; and I am glorified in them.

John 17:9,10

"I am Thine." You have said these words many, many times with no real conviction in your heart of what they meant. You are *beginning* to realize at a new level their awesome truth.

But now, My child, I say to you, "I am thine." This is no one-way relationship, but involves self-giving on both sides. Just as in marriage both must *give* and *receive*—so with our relationship. Before you are ready to say with "blessed assurance" that you are Mine, I had *given* Myself to you. In very truth, "I am thine."

June Eighth

Remember me, O Lord, when thou comest into Thy kingdom.

Luke 23:42

Your prayers are heard, My child, and they are stored up in My heart. Feeble though they are, and woefully imperfect, I do not despise nor reject them. My tender mercies are indeed over all My works, and I know your frame, that you are dust. But remember, My child, that My love is not like man's love. I love not only the brave and the beautiful. My heart goes out to all who truly seek after Me, however haltingly they walk. So keep on learning to pray—by praying. There is a world of wonder waiting to be discovered through prayer.

June Ninth

To the praise of the glory of His grace, where He hath made us accepted in the Beloved.

Ephesians 1:6

My works are mercy. My paths are peace. Your mind is still full of turbulence, because you still long for a false peace. The peace I give is not dependent on the favor or goodwill of others, and you must let go your demand that "they think well of you." For that demand has its own pain and sickness embedded in it.

I call you to My peace—a peace that passes understanding, a peace free from your life-long striving to be accepted by others. Know, My child, that I have accepted you and loved you with an everlasting love. You have not yet accepted My acceptance—and thereby have robbed yourself of much inner rest. Let them rest who hate you. It is not important that others love you. Blessings abound in the path I have chosen for you. My paths are peace, and My works are mercy.

June Tenth

And he said unto me, My grace is sufficient for thee: for My strength is made perfect in weakness.

II Corinthians 12:9

My strength is made perfect in weakness. This is an eternal truth, and you must learn what it means. I am mindful of your weakness, and your life is in My keeping. The days of your life are numbered—known to Me alone. You have seen that I am the repairer of ruins, the builder up of waste places. You do not have to understand "why" nor "how" this happens. What I call you to do is to rejoice in My works, to see and greet them for what they are.

Greater works are yet to unfold. My blessings are not running out, but they are for those who enter the secret place of My dwelling. Enter with Me every day. Guard the sacrifice as Abraham did of old. Be faithful to the end, and I will give you the crown of life.

June Eleventh

But I trust in thee, O Lord; I say, Thou art my God. My times are in Thy hand.

Psalm 31:14,15 (RSV)

I am the Lord in whose Hand are all the future years. Whatever disappointment or delay I allow to come into your plans and hopes, know of very truth that My way is best. I lead you along rough paths and smooth, green valleys and rugged mountains. I lead you toward the homeland I have prepared for you. The disappointments and sorrows are temporary, and they have their place in your pilgrimage. They wean you from false goals and steer you from wrong paths. Be not dismayed at bad tidings, for My eye is upon you and I will not leave nor forsake you.

June Twelfth

As sorrowful, yet always rejoicing; as poor, yet making many rich; as having nothing, and yet possessing all things.

II Corinthians 6:10

You are never nearer to Me than when your heart is overwhelmed with sorrow and uncertainty. You cannot fathom or understand this reality yet, My child, but you *can* accept it. My Spirit is given, not simply to give you times of joy and brightness, but to guide and lead you through the dark places.

Be of good cheer, and let no clouds keep you from embracing My blessings today, however they may come. Hold not back from those who reach out to you—make an extra effort to show your appreciation to them—for My sake. As surely as I am God, I will be with you. Count on it, build on it. I *am* with you always.

June Thirteenth

But God hath revealed them unto us by his Spirit: for the Spirit searcheth all things, yea, the deep things of God.

I Corinthians 2:10

I know your thoughts. Before you speak them, they are altogether known of Me. My Spirit searches the inner self (the inner man) and sees all. Your distractions, My child, are the fruit of your unfocused heart. You do not yet "will one thing" but try to fit many "goals" into your heart. It will not work. No rival can be allowed in the bride's heart if she is to welcome the Bridegroom. Your soul must be "centrified" in Me if you would taste the fullness of My blessing. I have given you a measure of stability—in spite of this unfocused condition. That is My grace. But I ask you to take much more seriously your need to "will one thing"—My will.

June Fourteenth

The Lord thy God in the midst of thee is mighty; He will save, He will rejoice over thee with joy; He will rest in His love; He will joy over thee with singing.

Zephaniah 3:17

My mercy is new every morning in hearts that seek Me. You can pray no better prayer than to entreat My mercy on those you love.

It is not that I *need* your prayers, My child, but that I allow you to participate in the *joy* of My goodness through your prayers. Your belief and your prayers *do* make a difference, for I have made a place for them in My plan.

Go now to your day with the full assurance that your prayer has been heard, and My mercy is renewed.

June Fifteenth

Wherefore, my beloved brethren, let every man be swift to hear, slow to speak, slow to wrath.

James 1:19

My child, My message today is this: watch your thoughts and your speech. They carry the potential of great harm. Be swift to hear and slow to speak—swift to hear any word against you, swift to hear the gentlest rebuke of My Spirit—and slow to speak the impulsive, critical thought that elevates you momentarily in your own eyes.

The race is not to the swift, nor the battle to the strong. Take your eyes off false goals. Let me lead you to the joys of My kingdom, where pride and place *have* no place, and where true rest is found even in the midst of work. That is what I offer you today—*today*—if you will listen to My voice and heed.

June Sixteenth

Thou tellest my wanderings: put Thou my tears in Thy bottle: are they not in Thy book?

Psalm 56:8

You are still a wandering sheep, scurrying about in your mind in various corners of My pasture. You still gaze out over the protective wall I have erected for your safety, and let your mind go after that which I have denied you. This inevitably brings turmoil and confusion when you could be advancing in a tranquil, settled stability. It is natural for lambs and young rams to gambol in playful wandering, but in maturity I expect more—a graver, more serious focus on the eternal verities I have revealed to you in My love. Let My word *dwell* in you richly as you choose to *dwell* in My will.

June Seventeenth

Who can utter the mighty acts of the Lord? Who can show forth all His praise?

Psalm 106:2

Praise My infinite compassion which I have freely bestowed on you. Praise befits the upright. Praise lifts up the spirit. Praise builds up faith. Praise defeats the enemy's stratagems. Praise joins your prayer to heaven, where My saints are already united in unending praise.

Earth's sorrows are but the backdrop against which the glory of My compassion shines. They cannot dim that glory in the heart that is filled with praise. Praise is a weapon too little appreciated and too little used by My people. I have given it as a gift and have long instructed that it be used. There are no obstacles that cannot be overcome. But My ways are not the ways of the world. Worldly wisdom will fail. But praise—true praise and persistent praise in the face of darkness—*will* prevail.

June Eighteenth

For whosoever shall save his life shall lose it; but whosoever shall lose his life for my sake and the Gospel's, the same shall save it.

Mark 8:35

My child, give over your desire to be liked or loved. You are much too easily affected by signs of being slighted. I have told you that I love you with an everlasting love. My love determines what I allow to come into your life. Yes, My *love* determines that, so be at peace and learn to love others with an undemanding, unself-conscious love, which I will give you—if you seek it sincerely and earnestly.

June Nineteenth

Thou art worthy, O Lord, to receive glory and honor and power; for thou hast created all things, and for Thy pleasure they are and were created.

Revelation 4:11

You are held in the Hand that holds the world. You are kept by the Power that rules the universe. I have said, "None can pluck you from My hand." It is not your feelings that keep you. It is not even your faith—for I know that waxes and wanes quickly under differing circumstances. No, it is My hand that holds you, My child, and protects you when you are least aware of it.

When your eyes are open and you are able to see this reality, give thanks and offer praise. When you cannot see or feel the reality, still give thanks and offer praise. That is an act of faith with which I am pleased. And by the exercise of your faith, it will grow stronger and steadier.

June Twentieth

If ye then, being evil, know how to give good gifts unto your children, how much more shall your Father which is in heaven give good things to them that ask Him?

Matthew 7:11

My heart is a free and ever-flowing heart of generous love. I take pleasure in doing good for My children. Beyond mere perfunctory gratitude for My gifts, I seek a relationship of unshakable trust in My goodness. I seek hearts that come to rest in My unfailing goodness. Those hearts cannot be shaken from their sure foundation by any change of circumstances. Circumstances do and must change, but My goodness changes not. This, My child, is what all My blessings and provisions are meant to effect—*your* unshakable faith in My unchanging goodness.

June Twenty–first

Out of Zion, the perfection of beauty, God hath shined.

Psalm 50:2

I take pleasure in providing blessings for My children. The beauty you see and enjoy is a gift of My love. You have a super abundance of it where I have placed and kept you. To enjoy it fully you must accept it as My gift of love. To reap all the benefits I intend, you must surrender your fretting. The earth is Mine and the fullness thereof. Do not lust after what I have denied you, but embrace what I have given so freely. I take pleasure in providing blessings for you, but I am saddened and grieved when you despise them and fail to recognize My fatherly care.

June Twenty–second

Ye ask, and receive not, because ye ask amiss, that ye may consume it upon your lusts.

James 4:3

Desires granted, desires denied—both flow from My sovereign will. You see and recognize My goodness in those I have granted. You do not yet see and recognize *clearly* My goodness in those I have denied. But it is all the same—My goodness at work for your good. It could not be otherwise, My child. Even now, as you wait long-delayed "answers" to your prayers, My work is still going on. Your faith is still weak and unstable. A small set-back throws it into confusion. My goal for you far exceeds what you can think or imagine. So do not spend time and energy mourning the loss of desires denied. Let them go in their time and be replaced by hopes that harmonize with My loving will.

June Twenty–third

And it shall come to pass, that like as I have watched over them, to pluck up, and to break down, and to throw down, and to destroy, and to afflict; so will I watch over them, to build, and to plant, saith the Lord.

Jeremiah 31:28

Yes, you need Me. I am your life, your breath, and you are sustained every moment by My power and My will. Not a sparrow falls without My permission. The world seems to be "out of control." But I have set limits on its freedom, and I keep faithful watch over My own. Yes, the world lies "in the power of the evil one"—through the disobedience and rebellion of My children. The way is still narrow that leads to life, and few there still are who find and follow it. Your little world is a small one, but My Spirit within is ever pushing out the borders to make room for My loving concern to live in you. Let this happen. Let pride and prejudice fall away, and see the beauty and joy of allowing My love to reign where your pettiness and self-righteousness ruled and crippled. Yes, My child, you need Me. I am your life, and will be your greater life—if you will.

June Twenty–fourth

The Lord did not set his love upon you, nor choose you, because you were more in number than any people; for ye were the fewest of all people: But because the Lord loved you.

Deuteronomy 7:7,8

My dear child, My love for you is sovereign and unchangeable. Your love for Me is fickle and erratic. Nevertheless, I tell you, My love is the firm foundation on which all your hope is founded—not your emotions or lack of them. Of My grace I give you to experience the feeling of love—the love My Spirit has shed abroad in your heart. But even when you feel arid and listless, My unchanging love is toward you.

I would have you grow in love and stability against the faithless fear that mars our relationship. You need much healing and deliverance there. It affects your relationships with others—not just with Me. I know your frame. I remember whence you came. I do not despise your beginnings nor reject you for your sins. My love is unchangeable. Let your love build on that.

June Twenty–fifth

The Lord seeth not as man seeth; for man looketh on the outward appearance, but the Lord looketh on the heart.

I Samuel 16:7

I know your heart better than you know it. I am acquainted with all its foibles and failings. I know its dark corners and its supreme concentration on itself. Yet I do not despise your cries and groans for greater stability and light. I have come to aid—to save—not to condemn. I am doing a work within, and you have My solemn, sovereign word: I will complete it. All I ask of you is that you continue to be open to Me, and follow through in obedience to My word. It shall be well with you, that I may be glorified.

June Twenty–sixth

Let us therefore cast off the works of darkness, and let us put on the armor of light.

Romans 13:12

As the light brings life to the earth, so My light brings life to your soul. My light banishes the darkness of hidden sin, the darkness of evil thoughts, the breeding places of soul-sickness and death.

Put away the works of darkness and choose the light-filled way. Let My sun drive out your dark and dank swamps of thought and feeling. Remember, My child, I am the Light of the world. Those who follow Me shall not walk in darkness but have the light of life. Leave the darkness—flee from it and hasten to Me.

June Twenty–seventh

Thou wilt show me the path of life; in Thy presence is fullness of joy; at Thy right hand there are pleasures evermore.

Psalm 16:11

I am your soul's delight. In My presence is *fullness* of joy. I give you, My child, a foretaste of heaven's pleasure when your heart floods with joy and thanksgiving. The road before you is purposely obscure. You do not need the burden of knowing the details. Grace abounds in each hard place, and I am with you in all you face. Keep your eyes on the goal—to finish the race and win the crown. The crown is for all who are faithful, not just a few. Keep listening to Me. That is important. You still have far to go to maintain a listening attitude. Your mind is still too cluttered with opinions and self-will. This is a training process I have brought you to. Be faithful and the fruit of it will be good. Delight in Me. My goodness is ever before you and never runs out.

June Twenty–eighth

And on the Sabbath we went out of the city by a riverside, where prayer was wont to be made.

Acts 16:13

My dear child, I am nearer than you think, more present to your mind and heart than you know. Your longings for unity and harmony are the fruit of My implanting. Let them encourage you to reach out in prayer for others, for prayers do make a difference. The world could be very different if My people had learned to pray. Your world and the world of those you love will be affected by your faithfulness or lack of faithfulness in prayer. The yearning you feel for "connectedness" is but a drawing of My Spirit toward the unity of spirit and harmony of heart which I will for My people. The place of prayer is a trysting place of the Spirit.

June Twenty–ninth

Brethren, I count not myself to have apprehended: but this one thing I do, forgetting those things which are behind, and reaching forth unto those things which are before, I press toward the mark for the prize of the high calling of God in Christ Jesus.

Philippians 3:13,14

This relationship of love has far to go. The distance is still there on your side. I draw near, but you recoil—still unwilling to risk all for the pearl of great price. I see you playing with the toys of jealousy, vanity, place, and pride. It grieves Me that you have learned so little and are still bound to the old feelings, nursing hurts and slights and being obnoxious withal. I have set you aside in many ways, to aid you in this process and show you the better way. As long as you hold on to your desire to "be somebody," you will suffer the inevitable consequences and miss My best for you. Come to Me, My child, and do not draw back. Let Me show My saving, healing power in the likes of you. You have nothing to lose but your pain.

June Thirtieth

Being found in fashion as a man, He humbled Himself and became obedient unto death, even the death of the cross.

Philippians 2:8

Dear to My heart are those who will follow Me in My humiliation. The world can still recognize goodness and self-denial, even though it loves evil and self-assertion. Those who will put down the secret longing to be lifted up in the eyes of others enter into a secret place where I love to abide.

The desire for recognition and appreciation still lives in your heart. I will aid you in mercy as you are willing to receive My aid, in putting this deadly desire to death. It *can* be done—and *will* be done if you are willing. Remember, the *desire* holds you back from Me. What folly, My child, to linger there when I hold out such a prize for you!

JULY

Charles Wesley
1707-1788

From every stormy wind that blows,
From every swelling tide of woes,
There is a calm, a sure retreat:
'Tis found beneath the mercy seat.

There is a scene where spirits blend,
Where friend holds fellowship with friend;
And heaven comes down our souls to greet
And glory crowns the mercy seat.

Talk with us, Lord, Thyself reveal,
While here o'er earth we rove;
Speak to our hearts, and let us feel
The kindling of Thy love.

Here then, my God, vouchsafe to stay,
And bid my heart rejoice;
My bounding heart shall own Thy sway,
And echo to Thy voice.

Thou callest me to seek Thy face,
'Tis all I wish to seek;
To hear the whispers of Thy grace,
And hear Thee inly speak.

July First

For my people have committed two evils: they have forsaken Me, the fountain of living waters, and hewed them out cisterns, broken cisterns, that can hold no water.

Jeremiah 2:13

My dear child, be content with My love. I see your heart still searching for others to love and respect you. Each time you go on such a search you are seeking vanity—emptiness. Do you not know that yet?

It grieves My heart to see My children, to whom I have revealed My mercy and lovingkindness so powerfully and clearly, still go "whoring" after emptiness. And so I ask you again, My child, be *content* with My love. It is enough, and you will come to see that it is more than you can ask or think. But it is seen and felt in its fullness only when you abandon the useless search for that which can never satisfy.

July Second

They shall ask the way to Zion with their faces thitherward, saying, "Come, and let us join ourselves to the Lord in a perpetual covenant that shall not be forgotten."

Jeremiah 50:5

My glory is seen in the mundane—the ordinary paths of the day. Look for Me more faithfully, My child, and you will surely meet Me there. Hidden from your eyes, I watch over you. Unseen, I protect and provide manifold blessings. Unthanked, I still provide.

You would be greatly blessed if you would cultivate and *practice* My presence more faithfully. My presence is there—*with* you. Did I not promise? "Lo, I am with you always, to the close of the age." That was not spoken just to the disciples on the Mount where I left them. It was My word to My people—those who come to Me and follow Me in their hearts. It is for you, My child, it is for you! How weak and foolish you are not to let Me be your constant Companion!

My glory *can* be seen in the ordinary paths. Will you look more faithfully?

July Third

According as He hath chosen us in Him before the foundation of the world, that we should be holy and without blame before Him in love.
Ephesians 1:4

My dear child, I speak to you in love. Your fear of what I might say grows out of an old, sick, and distorted view of Me and My relation to My children. You never ceased to love your own children, and you had no desire that fear of you would remain in that relationship. In like manner, the fear of the Lord is the *beginning* of wisdom, but "perfect love casts out fear." That means that as you mature, your only fear is that of offending or grieving My love—not the self-oriented fear of what I might *do* to you.

I speak to you in love because that is the essence of our relationship, from My perspective. I know that you still have far to go, but I do not despise you nor condemn you for it. Keep growing!

July Fourth

So shall my word be that goeth forth out of my mouth: it shall not return to me void, but it shall accomplish that which I please, and it shall prosper in the thing whereto I sent it.

Isaiah 55:11

I am the Bread of life. My very life is sustenance for your soul. I break the bread of My word, giving you your daily portion, sustaining you in your earthly journey. As the Israelites needed their daily supply of manna, so you *need* My freshly broken Bread.

My word does not return to Me empty. It produces the fruit of the Spirit in your soul. Bury it deeply by faith, so that its fruit may be abundant. I want your life to bear an abundant harvest. Remember, My child, that harvest comes toward the end of the year, and do not mourn that you will not see it all. Trust it to Me, and keep listening for My freshly broken word of life to you. That is more than enough.

July Fifth

For I am the Lord, I change not; therefore ye sons of Jacob are not consumed.

Malachi 3:6

I am with you today, My child, and you have nothing to fear. Go forth in the joy and anticipation of My blessing. Put aside needless worries and thoughts of what might be. They only tangle and crowd the path laid out before you. Be confident and of good courage, for the cause is Mine, not yours. I have promised and I will keep. There is not variableness or changing in Me. You shall yet see My hand at work to bring about My design and desire—so be prepared. Faith is the necessary key to unlock the treasury I have in store. I will help your unbelief if you will stay close to Me in your need.

July Sixth

Incline your ear and come unto me: hear and your soul shall live; and I will make an everlasting covenant with you, even the sure mercies of David.

Isaiah 55:3

Call upon Me and I will answer you. I have said this to you many times. It is enough that I have said it. You can build on that simple word. Call on Me and I will answer you. No one ever called on Me in vain.

Do not fear to come to Me in any condition. Do not let your sin deter your coming. I wait to be merciful. I am the Lord who forgives and heals. Do you not know that *I* know the condition in which you turn to Me? I read the thoughts and intentions of the heart. So do not be afraid of offending Me. Your separation from Me is more harmful than any sin you bring with repentance. Your safety is in staying close to Me.

July Seventh

For the Lord thy God bringeth thee into a good land, a land of brooks of water, of fountains and depths that spring out of valleys and hills.

Deuteronomy 8:7

Drink at the fountain of My love. Long your soul has dwelt in a dry and thirsty land. Drink and be renewed here where living water flows. I am the water of life, the living water that enlivens your dying soul. There can be no life apart from this living water.

I look for abundant growth. I see a soul still shrivelled and dry. I look for abundant fruit. I see but little, and the harvest is nigh. The need is great and the supply is unlimited. The day is still at hand, but night comes, when no man can work. Drink deeply, My child, at the fountain of My love—that your soul may be healed and your fruit may remain.

July Eighth

That they might be unto me for a people, and for a name, and for a praise, and for a glory. . . .

Jeremiah 13:11

Praise is My gift to you. As you lift your heart and voice to join the throngs of the ages, I give back to you far and above anything you can offer to Me. It is part of My sovereign plan that My children are blessed in blessing. When the whole creation shall praise its Creator and Redeemer, healing streams will flow through its veins, to keep it in perpetual health.

There can be no more healing prayer than praise—praise of the whole heart and soul. Praise of the body and voice. You are created as a whole person—and your praise *must* include body, soul, and spirit if it is to be complete. "Out of the mouths of babes Thou hast perfected praise"—why? Because in the simplicity of childhood, they hold nothing back out of "dignity" or "decorum."

My child, *learn* to praise Me more wholly. Praise is My gift to you.

July Ninth

And they heard the voice of the Lord God walking in the garden in the cool of the day; and Adam and his wife hid themselves from the presence of the Lord God amongst the trees of the garden.

Genesis 3:8

Again I tell you, I am the Lord who healeth thee. My promises are still in effect. I see your emotions vacillate between hope and despair. Your *fear* is your enemy. Remember, My child, perfect *love* casts out fear. There is *no* fear in love. I have not forgotten to be gracious. My heart is open to you. Your fear *closes* your heart to Me. You shall yet see the wonder of My grace. I have promised and I will be faithful. I have spoken and I will perform. It is not up to you to bring it about. This is My concern. Only believe! Only trust! Only confess your fear and flee to the Rock!

July Tenth

They looked unto Him, and were lightened; and their faces were not ashamed.

Psalm 34:5

My child, do not hurry. Wait for Me. Let the natural impatience of your soul be put to death by My delay. I know your need. You need not distress yourself. I always come on time. You will learn that if you will continue to wait on Me. I come laden with the gifts you need. Before you call, I am prepared with My answer. Yet your call is necessary, because you need to become needy in your own eyes.

Take your eyes off the circumstances that cause inner turmoil. Leave them to Me. Let My Spirit convict and convert your heart—not out of fear of what others may think or say or do—but in holy sorrow and compunction of heart toward Me. You have yet much to learn about true conviction, deep repentance, and the peace that forgiveness brings.

July Eleventh

One thing have I desired of the Lord, that will I seek after; that I may dwell in the house of the Lord all the days of my life, to behold the beauty of the Lord, and to inquire in His temple.

Psalm 27:4

Out of the deep you have called Me, and out of the deep I have answered you. Deep calleth unto deep. This is where I commune with you, when you turn and truly seek Me. You shall seek Me and find Me *when* you seek Me with all your heart. Deep unto deep.

Yes, you enter into the mystery of the ages, the communion of saints, the anteroom of heaven, when you seek and find Me here. You know the secret joy and strength which they found who have peopled these courts. A day in My courts is better than a thousand elsewhere.

It matters not what the outward surroundings are or were—palace or prison, temple or tabernacle. When My presence is truly sought and found, My glory fills the heart and that is enough.

July Twelfth

*And be ye kind to one another, tenderhearted, forgiving one another,
even as God for Christ's sake hath forgiven you.*

Ephesians 4:32

Come to Me with all your hurts and pain. Know that I the Lord
am with you and know each one. You can deal with them in self-pity,
deceiving yourself—or you can choose to let them crucify the self-love
that demands to be understood and agreed with. Stop defending
yourself. As soon as you feel misunderstood—stop. Take a breath
and pray to see—really see—the reality of the situation. Whether you
are "factually" right or not is not the important thing. The crucial
point is to see *into* the situation and take the other's point of view
seriously. You often misread this and provoke more conflict and more
pain. I will help you, but you must be willing to pay the price—and
for you, that is a costly one! But be of good cheer. The end is better
than the beginning.

My child, do not fret over the circumstances around you. Do not
allow the sin of others to draw you into judgment and self-righteousness.
Have mercy on them, as I have had mercy on you. Remember the story
of the servant who was forgiven a great debt, but acted unmercifully
toward a fellow-servant who owed him a small one. Do not magnify
the sin of others in your own mind, but "remember the rock from
which you were hewn and the pit from which you were digged."
That will enable you to "speak the truth in love" at the appointed
time.

July Thirteenth

Surely goodness and mercy shall follow me all the days of my life.

Psalm 23:6

I have magnified My mercy and will magnify it again. Goodness and mercy have followed you all the days of your life, and they shall follow you to the end. But do not presume, My child, on My mercy. Keep watch on the wayward side of your nature which the adversary is ever ready to exploit for his purposes. I do not want to see you hurt by any foolish choice, so My warning is against letting your joy in My mercy make you careless in this area. Being attentive to My presence is your safeguard.

July Fourteenth

The pride of thy heart hath deceived thee.

Obadiah vs. 3

I the Lord your God am speaking to you. Heaven and earth shall pass away—but My love is eternal. My child, you still have far to go and much to receive before the fullness of this truth is in you. You still operate on the basis of merit and punishment—of being good and being bad. You still take pride in the works of My grace, and do not pay the fullness of tribute to Me. The momentary lift you get from such pride comes with a high price. It damages your soul and delays your progress toward maturity. Learn to recognize these feelings and *quickly* bring them to Me before great damage is done, and you find yourself in enemy territory. It can be done. It is not without hope of change, even though your nature is badly bent in this pattern. Credit and glory are not the true fulfillment you have thought them to be. They are chains that bind you to a changing, dying, fickle world. But you *can* break the chains!

July Fifteenth

And let us not be weary in well doing: for in due season we shall reap, if we faint not.

Galatians 6:9

My dear child, wait awhile. Do not be impatient when you do not see an immediate answer to your prayers. Waiting is an important part of the prayer process. It is a great separator of the trivial from the heartfelt request. It is a time for refining of motives in asking. It is an *active* time, not merely an unwanted delay.

Wait awhile. My ears are open to your needs and the needs of those you hold before Me. No prayer is wasted. In My love, I take them into account and turn them to good effect, even when the answer is not what you hoped or wanted. Knowing that secret, pray on—and wait awhile. You will have ample cause to rejoice.

July Sixteenth

And He said, Draw not nigh hither: put off thy shoes from off thy feet, for the place whereon thou standest is holy ground.

Exodus 3:5

In the midst of trouble and uncertainty, I am still your peace. This is the peace that passes all understanding, because it is not tied to nor dependent on the pleasantness of the circumstances of your life. I know the situation you face. I am still Lord of it. What I ask of you is to draw near to Me and stay near to Me "until this storm be overpast." Have I not promised to be with you in trouble? Is My arm shortened that it cannot save? Turn from the fear and unbelief that arise in your heart at the first sign of trouble. Call upon Me and I will answer you. Learn, learn, learn to trust Me—and go forward with Me. Today's Scripture is not there by accident or "coincidence." "Take your shoes off your feet, for the ground on which you stand is holy." That means the *foundation* on which you stand in Me is holy ground. Believe it and do not fear!

July Seventeenth

For all people will walk every one in the name of his god, and we will walk in the name of the Lord our God for ever and ever.

Micah 4:5

Walk in the light that you have, My child, and do not let the darkness draw you away from Me. The way is still narrow and the darkness is still great, but there is light enough on your path. Day will come, but for this time, these shadows remain. *Quit you like a man*, and strive against the enemy and his forces—they war for your soul. You do not have to be strong, but you must stay in the path of light to be safe.

July Eighteenth

I have set before you life and death, blessing and cursing; therefore choose life, that both thou and thy seed may live.

Deuteronomy 30:19

It is all in My hands—your welfare and your future. You are right to rejoice in My mercy, for My mercy is from everlasting to everlasting. Those who taste My mercy have reason to rejoice with exceeding great joy.

My heart is made glad when you begin to move from low thoughts and desires and yearn for heavenly things. I will not force this move on you or anyone, because I have created you with the gift of choice. Choose life, My child, choose life. Choose the higher life—the life I offer you each day, instead of groveling in your own thoughts and desires. Your welfare and your future are in My hands *if* you leave them there. *That* is your "door of hope" in the valley of Achor—an open door. Come through it.

July Nineteenth

Great peace have they which love Thy law; and they shall have no stumbling block.

Psalm 119:165

It is good to wait in My presence. You are being blessed and fed by My Spirit, even when you hear no words. It is good to keep trusting when your prayers are delayed. You have been long in coming to this place, and there is still much ground to reclaim. You have built a fortress around your mind, and trusted in your own thoughts and opinions rather than on Me. They failed you when great need arose, and you were faced with their inability to help. I have not failed you, but you forfeited much peace by your choices. It is good to wait in My presence. This, too, is part of My work to help you regain and reclaim lost ground.

July Twentieth

Honor and majesty are before Him: strength and beauty are in His sanctuary.

Psalm 96:6 (RSV)

The riches of My Word are hidden from the natural eye. It sees the outer "shell" and may even admire what it sees. But to those who are willing to ask, to seek and to knock, My treasury unlocks its greater beauty. Here the soul feasts, and here it finds joys which it cannot describe. Truly, My child, those who find these riches can say, "The lines have fallen to me in pleasant places. I have a goodly heritage." The beauty of holiness is seen and experienced in the garden of love. The glimpses you are given of My beauty and glory are gifts to help you through your hard times. Treasure them and do not forget them.

July Twenty–first

Let us lift up our hearts with our hands unto God in the heavens.

Lamentations 3:41

Lift up your heart! Look to Me and for Me throughout this day. My love does not waver or vacillate. Through the darkest times, My light does not diminish or go out. Only your perception of it changes.

Lift up your heart! Be of good cheer, and do not fear the future. By faith embrace the future as I unfold it. Leave to Me what I design to accomplish with the circumstances you dread. Leave it to Me to turn evil to good. Learn, learn, learn that most important clue to uniting with Me when your understanding is failing you miserably. I will meet you there, and *together* we will walk through the hard places.

Lift up your heart and be of good cheer. My yoke is still easy and My burden is still light.

July Twenty–second

They that sow in tears shall reap in joy.

Psalm 126:5

The early rain and the latter rain—tears given to water the dry ground of your soul. The early rains were the tears that came in your youth, though you were embarrassed by them and did not understand what they were doing. But they opened the ground of your soul to receive impressions of My Spirit and the seed of My Word to grow silently therein. The latter rain is your present gift, again to enable your soul to receive My life-giving Word. Do not despise the tears, and do not try to delve into secrets hidden from you. Let My word grow to bring forth an abundant harvest.

July Twenty–third

But God forbid that I should glory, save in the cross of our Lord Jesus Christ, by whom the world is crucified unto me, and I unto the world.
Galatians 6:14

My child, I will keep you in the cross—in the life-giving sacrifice of My child on Calvary. Mercy flows even yet from that life-giving source. Your life is there, hidden in the mystery of My suffering. Let it break your stony, rebellious heart to know the price I paid for you—yes, My child, for *you*. These are not empty words; these are from your Father's heart.

Let the world pass by with its glory and its shame. Your life—your true life—is here, at the place of sacrifice. Bathe your spirit in the life-giving stream of mercy. Drink from the life-giving stream of mercy. Look deeply into the unfathomable depths of mercy—and let your spirit, your heart, your soul be changed.

July Twenty–fourth

Behold, I stand at the door and knock: if any man hear my voice and open the door, I will come in to him, and will sup with him, and He with me.
Revelation 3:20

My dear child, why is it so hard for you to accept My words of love? Or the reality of My love for you? Have I not proved over and over that I love you with a supernatural and unfailing love? Has My care ever been lacking? Yet you draw back, frightened, guilty, defensive—even against Me.

I will not force Myself beyond that inner citadel. I stand at the door and knock—for My nature is to respect what I have created and given life to. When I said "We will come in and sup with him," I meant that a whole world of friendship awaits those who hear My voice and allow Me free entrance to the inmost recesses. It is Love that stands—that pleads. Let Me take full charge. Don't let pride, fear, jealousy or any shame keep Me from Love's goal. My dear child, why do you think I died for you?

July Twenty–fifth

The blood of Jesus Christ cleanseth us from all sin.

I John 1:7

The wounds of the soul must be cleansed before healing can take place. The cleansing process is painful for you, because the stains are the result of your sinful choices in the past. The more you are aware of this, the easier it makes your cooperation with the process. The light of truth exposes the ugliness of these sores, but the Balm of Gilead then restores lost beauty. Marvel at the goodness that directs My operation, and do not flinch at the necessary pain.

July Twenty–sixth

I will cause the shower to come down in its season; there shall be showers of blessing.

Ezekiel 34:26

I shower upon you the showers of mercy. Forget not all My benefits, My child, for in forgetting you sever yourself from the life-giving water and become arid and fruitless. Abundant grace is always available to you—and remembering prompts you to take hold of it.

My plans for you still move forward. You are not forgotten, and no prayer is prayed in vain when it comes from a repentant, remembering heart. So I bid you again, forget not all My benefits. They are more than the stars in heaven.

July Twenty–seventh

For we have not an high priest which cannot be touched with the feeling of our infirmities; but was in all points tempted like as we are, yet without sin.

Hebrews 4:15

Hidden in the mystery of My love are all the events of your life, good and bad. Have I not said, "As far as the east is from the west, so far have I removed your transgression from Me"? This is not an empty phrase. It is a proclamation of divine mercy to helpless sinners. Forgiveness is the key that unlocks My fulfillment—forgiving those who have wronged or hurt you and *accepting* forgiveness for the wrongs you have committed.

My dear Son entered into the darkest valley of suffering to change the power of guilt into the power of forgiveness. My people know little—almost nothing—of what He accomplished there. Enter into this truth as you have never done and invite others to venture in. In doing so, you enter further into My heart.

July Twenty–eighth

The Spirit searcheth all things, yea, the deep things of God.
I Corinthians 2:10

In your dreams I have spoken, and in dark language I have communicated with your spirit. You do not have to understand with your rational mind all that I am doing. You need only to be obedient to that which I clearly speak.

There are depths in the human heart which can be plumbed only by My Spirit. The heart is a deep cavern, and there are many hiding places where sin lurks undetected. The confusions you feel come from these smelly places, and the Spirit seeks them out as you cease resisting Him. "Truth in the inward parts" comes by the Spirit of Truth occupying and enlightening those hidden places.

July Twenty–ninth

And He said unto me, My grace is sufficient for thee: for my strength is made perfect in weakness. Most gladly therefore will I rather glory in my infirmities, that the power of Christ may rest upon me.

II Corinthians 12:9

"My grace is sufficient for you. My strength is made perfect in weakness." Your weakness is a necessary part of our relationship, for your strength would vie with Me if I allowed it to prevail. Your weakness is a gift of safety—to keep you from veering too far from the path of My will. Yes, in years past, My child, your weakness was used to prevent your leaving here. So there is not cause for recrimination against yourself or others—but rather an inner reconciliation between the outer circumstances and inner circumstances of your life.

Rejoice in My grace more and more. It is not an excuse for passivity or sin, but it is a fountain of refreshment and renewal. It is a life-giving cordial, a continuing cause of wonder and gratitude to My children. Since it is *reality*, it cannot lead you astray. I am the God of grace!

July Thirtieth

And after the earthquake a fire; but the Lord was not in the fire: and after the fire a still small voice.

I Kings 19:12 (RSV)

I the Lord your God am with you, My child. Walk this day with Me, consciously seeking to hear and heed "the still small Voice" of My Spirit within your heart. I will speak to you and guide you. Only be careful to listen!

You cannot know the way or the path to follow on your own. Confusion is sown by the adversary to trap the unwary. But I have promised, and My promise is faithful, that I will show the path through the maze.

Your faith will be strengthened if you will be careful to heed My words. You will grow more confident in this new walk, and that is good. I want your faith to become more simple and ready to act. Are you sufficient for this? No, but remember, My child, your sufficiency will be of *Me*. And there is no lack there!

July Thirty–first

The Lord is my light and my salvation; whom shall I fear? the Lord is the strength of my life; of whom shall I be afraid?

Psalm 27:1

Light rises in the dark places when they are opened to My presence. Light dispels the negative and gloomy thoughts and feelings, and scatters the shadows of night. I am the Daystar, the Light-giver who brings hope and gladness to your soul. Welcome Me, My child, with a wide open door—for I come bearing precious gifts. You are not called to dwell in sadness or to pine for those things that cannot be. Let their absences free you to see the wonders I have to unfold before you, and be fully present to them. Trust Me to guide your way, to guard what you have entrusted to Me, to keep you and your loved ones safe from harm—and let My joy be your strength.

AUGUST

Fanny Crosby
1820-1915

Thy Holy Spirit, Lord, alone

Can turn our hearts from sin;
His power alone can sanctify
And keep us pure within.

Thy Holy Spirit, Lord, can bring
The gifts we seek in prayer;
His voice can words of comfort speak
And still each wave of care.

Thy Holy Spirit, Lord, can give
The grace we need this hour;
And while we wait, O Spirit, come
In sanctifying power.

August First

Come unto me, all ye that labor and are heavy laden, and I will give you rest.

Matthew 11:28

I am your Father and your Savior. There is no reason to be cut off from Me. I have called you and I will sustain you to the end. O ye of little faith! How many times have I revealed My tender mercies to you—and yet you fear! Be done with living in the shadows when My light is shining for you. I tell you again: life is to be *lived,* not simply endured. Do not be afraid to reach out, to share your life with others, to extend My blessing to them. I will show you and direct you as you obey. Only *do* live, My child, and learn to trust.

August Second

Jesus said, Have faith in God. What things soever ye desire, when ye pray, believe that ye receive them, and ye shall have them. And when ye stand praying, forgive.

Mark 11:22,24,25

There are no restrictions to limit the extent of your faith in Me. I have not set bounds on what I am able to do in response to the prayer of faith. The limits you put on it are your own, and they do limit the extent and outreach of your prayers. That is a spiritual law which operates for every child of Mine.

Just as muscles atrophy or grow with disuse or use, so faith dwindles or grows with exercise. I seek vigorous, faith-filled children who, like Gideon, in spite of fear, went ahead and dared to trust Me. Your fear restricts, while faith releases. It is a barrier to be overcome if you are to move in the glorious liberty of the children of God. Why wait?

August Third

Exhorting one another: and so much the more, as ye see the day approaching.

Hebrews 10:25

In the early morning light, there is hope for greater light. Shadows flee before the rising sun. Even so, My child, the glimmers of your "early morning light" hold the promise of a clearer day. Shadows of doubt and fear, guilt and sin cannot stand before My light. I am your light and your promise that hope will not be disappointed. You have light enough for every step of today's journey. Rejoice in it, be thankful for it, and you will see that I *am* the Way, the Truth and the Life.

August Fourth

Henceforth there is laid up for me a crown of righteousness, which the Lord, the righteous judge, shall give me at that day; and not to me only, but unto all them also that love His appearing.

II Timothy 4:8

Crowns and honors are Mine to give. They are never to be sought for their own sake. My glory is seen in those who do not seek their own. They are blessed with the secret joy which I impart to the humble. Seek humility, My child, as a treasure more precious than gold. Do not despise the humiliations I send or allow, for they are sharp instruments to prune away the rank overgrowth of pride. Look about you and see the signs that I am at work on your proud nature, to make humility a possibility for you. That is a token of My love.

August Fifth

For evildoers shall be cut off: but those that wait upon the Lord, they shall inherit the earth.

Psalm 37:9

Blessed are those who wait for Me. My coming is always on time, but to you it may seem too long delayed. In the waiting, your desire is tested. I have told you to ask, seek, and knock—to keep on asking, seeking, knocking—for in that process a winnowing is taking place, and the depth of your desire is seen. Distractions offer relief from waiting, so beware the subtlety of their appeal. Fight to stay in focus. I have not abandoned you, and My purpose is still for your good. Remember that always—always, My child. My love for you is an everlasting, eternal love.

August Sixth

He turneth the wilderness into a standing water, and dry ground into watersprings.

Psalm 107:35

My way is in the desert, My child, where hidden springs flow and unexpected oases appear. The desert is the dryness and separateness you feel. You lose sight of the path, you lose sight of the goal of your journey, and you lose sight of the meaning of your days. My oases appear and you are again refreshed, but you cannot stay in that pleasant resting place. My way is in the desert and through the desert—toward your true destination and home. Trudge on, but do not forget your Companion on the way. The journey is not over. The end is not yet.

August Seventh

Take no thought for the morrow: for the morrow shall take thought for the things of itself. Sufficient unto the day is the evil thereof.

Matthew 6:34

Do not worry, do not worry, do not worry! I am He who holds your life in My hand. All is well and shall be well, My child, for I am God. You shall still see My glory revealed, and there *will* be a fulfillment of all I have spoken to you.

August Eighth

In Him was life; and the life was the light of men. And the light shineth in the darkness.

John 1:4,5

Many hues are contained in the sunbeams you see. In like manner, My light contains blessings of many kinds. Some of them you can recognize and enjoy. Others are not visible to your sight or mind, but they work invisibly in the soul to accomplish My purpose. The entrance of My word gives light.

My child, darkness is the absence of light. When darkness threatens your tranquillity, remember that Light dispels darkness—and yours is the responsibility to seek it, and keep on seeking it until the shadows flee before it. You prefer darkness when your heart has turned from Me. Choose light.

August Ninth

The voice of Thy thunder was in the heaven: the lightnings lightened the world: the earth trembled and shook.

Psalm 77:18

My thoughts come to you in the midst of your thoughts. Because you are still bound by your old habits, you do not recognize or greet them. I still choose to speak in the "still, small voice" rather than the thunder. My yoke is easy. I am gentle and lowly of heart. But because I love you and care for your welfare, I *will* speak in thunder if necessary. So tune your heart to hear. Be assured that the Voice is there, and that it *is* possible to commune with Me more consistently than you have ever known.

August Tenth

But the Lord is faithful, who shall establish you, and keep you from evil.

II Thessalonians 3:3

My child, do not fret yourself because of evil doers. They are Mine to deal with, and I am aware of the condition of their hearts.

My mantle of mercy is still over the work of My hands, and you need not fear the evil day. Have I not told you?

I want to see more joy, more faith, more freedom in My children. I want you all to *rejoice* in your salvation which has been achieved at so great a price. As long as you allow fear and foreboding to prevail, you refuse the abundant life I have given you. Obedience and joy must kiss each other. Put off the old garment of doubt and put on the new garment of joy and praise.

August Eleventh

Godliness with contentment is great gain.

I Timothy 6:6

Hear My voice, My child. I speak in the depths. I know your fear and worries, and I am acquainted with your thoughts. Much of your energy is wasted in wounded pride and thwarted dreams. You have not yet fully submitted yourself to My mild yoke, and in your rebellion you have carved a harder one for yourself. Accept My love as I have given it to you. Accept My blessings as I have poured them out on you. Remember that gratitude and grumbling cannot dwell together. Choose which shall reign in the depths of your heart and soul.

August Twelfth

Humble yourselves therefore under the mighty hand of God, that He may exalt you in due time.

I Peter 5:6

Holy, Holy, Holy is the Lord God of Hosts. I dwell in the high and holy place, and seek a dwelling place on earth among the lowly. I am grieved at the ingratitude which allows your heart to close itself from Me. I am merciful and full of compassion, but I am the Holy One. Lose no time in turning to Me, and learn to avoid the ways that lead to darkness and death. You were created for *life*. Embrace My life more fully today, My child.

August Thirteenth

. . . and again I say, Rejoice.

Philippians 4:4

Rejoice, My child, rejoice. Let praise fill your heart and overflow from your life. Believe in the efficacy of prayer—even your own feeble ones. My ear is open even to the sighs of My children. While you wait to see the changes prayer can bring about, rejoice in faith and drive away the scavengers of doubt that would take away your sacrifice of praise. Praise and faith strengthen and nourish one another.

That is why Paul says, "With thanksgiving let your requests be made known to God."

August Fourteenth

They looked unto Him and were lightened, and their faces were not ashamed.

Psalm 34:5

Lift up your hands and your heart to Me and expect My word to be fulfilled. The great sin and barrier to your prayers is your lack of expectant faith. You entertain doubts and accusing thoughts without realizing their true nature and the danger they pose to your welfare. I bid you to believe, but I will not force you to believe. That I have reserved for you. It is a choice, and if you will make it against your fearful thoughts and feelings, you will see its fruit. Leave the hard questions aside, and come as a little child to Me.

August Fifteenth

. . . Christ Jesus came into the world to save sinners, of whom I am chief.
I Timothy 1:15

I am full of truth and grace. The record of the years will testify to My goodness and mercy. My will and intention for you has never changed. It is to bring you out of your fickleness and folly into the likeness of My child. When the task is complete, you will be able to see what is now hidden from your eyes—My mercy at work at all times—even when you were farthest from Me. You still want to take credit, and you still think you are better than others. Pray for courage to face the truth and for gratitude that you have been kept by My sovereign power from yourself.

August Sixteenth

. . . I am He who searcheth the reins and hearts.

Revelation 2:23

Your days are based on anxiety and fear. These in turn are rooted in pride, fear of looking bad to others. My days bring peace. My timetable is always sufficient to accomplish what I require. Let My peace stand guard over your mind, and let your anxious thoughts fade away like the morning dew. O foolish and slow of heart to believe! Have I not always been faithful? Give over the reins, My child, give them over that peace may prevail.

August Seventeenth

But avoid foolish questions, and genealogies, and contentions, and strivings about the law; for they are unprofitable and vain.

Titus 3:9

Take heed and beware of foolish arguments. They foment strife and division of spirit. Restrain your strong, natural impulse to push for your own ideas and opinions. Learn to be quiet. Learn to leave to Me the settling of great questions and small ones. Seek peace and pursue it. In your weakness My strength can and will prevail. In your strength, you nullify Mine. This is an important step which I am offering you, and I will help you if you will heed My word.

August Eighteenth

So great a cloud of witnesses . . .

Hebrews 12:1

My dear child, My mercy-seat is always open to you. Here you are surrounded by many who have frequented it before you. You are not aware of their presence or their aid in your journey, but they are partners with you in the struggle you face.

Be not afraid to embrace new understandings as you journey with Me. New scenes and new occasions have their place in your growth. You are reluctant to give up old ideas and habits, even as you try new ones. You still fear what others will think about you. But remember how steady My mercy has been, and do not fear to widen the scope of your spiritual vision—it is safe here at the mercy-seat.

August Nineteenth

With the merciful Thou wilt show Thyself merciful.

Psalm 18:25

I have this against you, My child, that you show so little mercy to those who need it most. Mercy is not softness nor compromise with truth, but truth without mercy can be hard and sharp. It can build walls when bridges are needed.

As I rehearse the many examples and instances of My mercy to you, remember the parable of the servant who would not forgive the debt of his fellow-servant. Learn from this that I intend My mercy to be multiplied through you to others. Be not deceived nor think of yourself more highly than you ought to think. While there is yet time, ask for guidance and set your heart to learn and practice being a mercy-giver.

August Twentieth

And I will give thee the treasures of darkness, and hidden riches of secret places, that thou mayest know that I, the Lord, which call thee by thy name, am the God of Israel.

Isaiah 45:3

Blessed are those who listen, for they shall hear. Blessed are those who hear, for they shall know. I am known of those who listen and those who heed. My heart is open to those who seek Me, and I never refuse those who come to Me.

I have moved your heart to yearn for Me, and denied you the satisfactions that would have falsely sated your hunger. That thirst you feel for a closer companionship with Me is meant to keep you dissatisfied with anything less. Do not look for full satisfaction here in any earthly relationship or any place. Only in Me, My child, is your true home and goal. Journey on.

August Twenty–first

Lo, I am with you always, even unto the end of the world.

Matthew 28:20

I go before you, My child, and prepare the way. When you walk in My way, your life fulfills My purpose for you. When you follow your own path, the results are dead and lifeless. Redeem the time,

My child. These days have been given for purposes you cannot fully see nor understand. Yours is not to view the distant scene, but to stay close to Me and let My will prevail. That is reward enough for now, and there is much to do.

August Twenty–second

Who forgiveth all thine iniquities; who healeth all thy diseases.
                                                          Psalm 103:3

My child, I am still healing ancient wounds in your soul. The process is slow and often hidden from your view. But I tell you, of a truth, it is taking place. You are not marking time and your circumstances are not accidents. So lift up your head and your heart, and receive each day as a gift. You do not know the end, but I do, and I am leading you toward My goal for you.

August Twenty–third

Yea, though I walk through the valley of the shadow of death, I will fear no evil; for Thou art with me.
                                                          Psalm 23:4

My dear child, I have no delight in the suffering of My people. I allow it only for their eternal good. Blessed are those who turn to Me in their trouble, for I am a God of mercy and compassion. The valleys through which I call you to go need not frighten you. The shadows and darkness are only for a time. Let your faith grow strong when darkness comes. Faith will overcome where daylight cannot prevail. Suffering purges away the rank growth of self—if you let it do its work. There are two ways in which I turn it to good: by its pruning and by My healing. In both ways I bring blessing to My chosen ones.

August Twenty–fourth

My times are in Thy hand: deliver me from the hand of mine enemies. Save me for Thy mercies' sake.

Psalm 31:15,16

Your prayers are heard, My child, and you need not fear. Hold fast to what you know, to My dealings and the revealings of My heart to you. These are steady lodestars by which to chart your course. You need not fear what lies ahead, because I always prepare the way for you. When you walk with Me, no harm can come to you. The only danger you have to face is your own unstable and unfaithful nature. That requires diligence and a readiness to confront its twists and turns.

August Twenty–fifth

For the Lord God is a sun and shield: the Lord will give grace and glory: no good thing will He withhold from them that walk uprightly.

Psalm 84:11

No good thing have I withheld from you, My child. In My wisdom and mercy, I have not allowed you to have many things you wanted, but their denial was a blessing, not a curse. I have showered My gifts on you—in part, because of the frailty and difficulty of your nature. The abundance of My mercy toward you is better than the abundance you could have gathered with a more attractive and winsome nature. The brokenness you have carried inside is a necessary part of this gift, so that it may yet bear the fruit and harvest I intend for it. In the meantime, let it all work its work in your soul and give thanks!

August Twenty–sixth

Thy righteousness is like the great mountains; Thy judgments are a great deep.

Psalm 36:6

The depths of My love you cannot know as long as you cling to your old life. There are many overt and subtle ways of clinging. You are loathe to give up the little comforts and satisfactions, fleeting though they be. But they exact a price all out of keeping with their reward. You must become more aware of their temptation, for you too easily give in without a thought of their real and destructive nature. Your mind is a mine field. Your thoughts are weapons in the hand of the adversary, and you do not even recognize them as such. I do not want you to become super-spiritual and unnatural. I do not call you to weirdness. Rather to awareness—full consciousness of the reality of the warfare which is in your life. If you will choose this, I will help you. If you refuse it, you will suffer great loss.

August Twenty–seventh

The Lord hath been mindful of us: He will bless us; He will bless the house of Israel; He will bless the house of Aaron. He will bless them that fear the Lord, both small and great.

Psalm 115:12,13

Your knowledge of Me is grounded in My dealings with you. I am mindful of you, even when you are not mindful of Me. I am at work in the circumstances and consciences of those for whom you pray. You do not yet realize the power of prayer nor its place in My universe. You have only "tapped the surface" of prayer as yet. But I give you indications, "earnests," to show that I am in your prayers and that I move you to pray. As you obey My Spirit you come to a fuller, firmer knowledge of Me, and are blessed. I am ever mindful of you, My child.

August Twenty–eighth

Therefore with joy shall ye draw water out of the wells of salvation.
Isaiah 12:3

Draw near to Me, My child, and I will not fail to draw near to you. You never seek Me in vain, no matter what your feelings tell you. I, the Lord, change not. My face is ever toward you for good even when you are least aware of it.

Out of the well of salvation comes the water of life. Drink deeply of this life-giving Spirit, My child, that you may be a conveyor of that water to others. Look for opportunities to witness to My goodness to others, and deny the negative spirit.

August Twenty–ninth

But I fear, lest by any means, as the serpent beguiled Eve through his subtlety, so your minds should be corrupted from the simplicity that is in Christ.

II Corinthians 11:3

I am nearer than breathing, closer than hands and feet. I am *within,* though you know it not. When you listen, My child, listen within, where Spirit communes with spirit. Do not doubt and mistrust what you hear. Doubt drives a wedge between your spirit and Mine. It is the work of the adversary of your soul, to prevent you from entering into the fullness of your birthright. "The simplicity that is in Christ" is here—Christ in you, the hope of glory.

August Thirtieth

. . . my strength is made perfect in weakness.

II Corinthians 12:9

My dear child, calm yourself at My breast. Let your faint knowledge of Me give you strength for your needs. I am enough—sufficient for any circumstance you are called to face. There is *always* within the circumstance grace to bear it and a way through.

I have not called you to walk a blind path, even though the future is unknown to you. I have called you to walk *with* Me, and I tell you again, I am enough—sufficient for any circumstance you are called to face. No exceptions!

August Thirty–first

Thou hast set my feet in a large room.

Psalm 31:8

A certain man lived in a large, beautiful mansion. It was made of stone and was built to last indefinitely. The house was occupied by a suitable staff of servants, ready to supply his every need. From time to time people would pass by and comment on the beauty and stability of the house, and would wonder what it was like inside. One thing they noticed: a small, rather unsightly path made its way across the lawn to a back servants' entrance. And the man, the owner, always approached his home via this path and through this door. What others did not know was that the man, the owner of this large, beautiful stone mansion, lived in one small servant's room in the back of the house. It had been so long since he even visited the other rooms that he couldn't remember what they looked like, and felt no sense of identity as their owner. Nor did he call on his servants to help him. Instead, he went in and out, afraid of losing his little servant's room, and angry that he found life so dull and uninteresting. He was very conscious of his aches and pains, his changing moods, and often retired to his room hurt and angry at what others said or thought.

Let those hear who have ears to hear. . . .

SEPTEMBER

Speak, Lord, in the stillness,
  While I wait on Thee;
Hushed my heart to listen
  In expectancy.

Speak, O blessed Master,
  In this quiet hour,
Let me see Thy face, Lord,
  Feel Thy touch of power.

For the words Thou speakest-
  "They are life" indeed;
Living Bread from heaven,
  Now my spirit feed.

E. May Grimes Crawford
1864-1927

September First

Blessed are they that mourn, for they shall be comforted.

Matthew 5:4

Mourn your sins, My child, for blessed are they that mourn. You shall be comforted even as you face the pain. My work is going on. You cannot see nor understand the depth of it, but I assure you that it is in process. Nothing is static and nothing is condemned to stay the same. That is an illusion of this earth, and you must seek to see the reality beneath. In order to cooperate with My will, you must choose to loose yourself from such illusions, and embrace My will for today— and by faith, for the future. Do not hang on to the past, bad or good. Go forward with Me into My future.

September Second

Is not My word like as a fire? saith the Lord; and like a hammer that breaketh the rock in pieces?

Jeremiah 23:29

My word is like a hammer, breaking up the hardened crust of your heart. I want you to have a tender, *feeling* heart, able to be touched with the pain and sorrow of others. You have built up walls of deadness around your heart to protect you from pain and to avoid looking weak. Your weakness, My child, is My gift to you. Your strength is your rejection of that gift. There is a world of difference between your strength and Mine. I will show you that difference when this breaking and hammering have done their work.

September Third

And He said unto me, My grace is sufficient for thee.
                                                    II Corinthians 12:9

Yes, My child, I am here. My grace is sufficient for you and for all those you love. Trust Me in this present circumstance. I have not forgotten to be gracious! Each uncertain hour is an opportunity for you to praise My goodness—even before you see the outworking of it before your eyes.

Call upon Me more faithfully and fervently, not for My sake but for yours. I know your needs and I am at work to meet them, but you need the exercise of prayer to be ready for My blessing. Do not think the time is wasted that you spend in prayer. Prayer is an antidote to pride and self-generated activity. Beware of the stress of busyness that crowds out the call to turn aside to be with Me. Back to basics.

September Fourth

But the sorrow of the world worketh death.

II Corinthians 7:10

Ah! My child, you grieve over many things—foolish things that have not ultimate meaning. Repent of your haughty attitude when you are crossed in your opinions. This quality of yours is offensive to others and to Me. The only way out is humiliation—the bitter cure for such ailments. It *is* an ailment and an old condition—and for your own sake, it must yield. Once you have agreed with Me to let it fall, I will be near to help. What you are guarding is not worth the effort or the pain—pain for yourself and for others. So take courage and go forward.

September Fifth

But the land whither ye go to possess it, is a land of hills and valleys.

Deuteronomy 11:11

My dear child, the valleys as well as the hills are Mine. Do not wonder that your path takes the lowlands as well as the high. I am with you in the desert as well as in the garden. To know this is life indeed.

Be not afraid of tomorrow. All your tomorrows are known and planned by Me—the Architect of time. I know the plans I have for you, plans of good and not of evil. Let your heart be open to My goodness.

September Sixth

For it is a good thing that the heart be established with grace.
                                                                    Hebrews 13:9

Hearken to Me, My child, and I will speak with you. Quell the busy, wandering thoughts and center your mind on Me. Only thus can you hear a clear and undistorted word from Me.

The work of renewal and revision is far from done. In each one of you, I am seeking to do a new thing. Yes, "seeking," because I require the willing consent and assent of My children in order to carry on My work within. This will not be easy, because an easier, less demanding way has been followed. Truth in the inward parts does not come without a price. Only those willing to pay the price will receive the prize.

Continue to seek Me and My truth for your life. Do not let circumstances become an excuse to let up in this task. Have I not rewarded your efforts far beyond any expectation? Let these past months be a foundation for future faithfulness to our mutual goal—and the process by which you will move toward it.

September Seventh

And he saith unto me, "Write: Blessed are they which are called unto the marriage supper of the Lamb."

Revelation 19:9

Happy are those who are invited to the marriage supper of the Lamb—a foretaste of that glory I give to My children in quiet moments of fellowship with Me. I have promised and My promises are yea and amen. I *will* come in and sup with them and they with me.

Happy are those whose sins are forgiven, whose iniquity is covered. Tears of repentance mingle with those of joy at My mercies, for to repent of sin is to know My mercy in a new and fresh way. Thankfulness and obedience grow from this seedbed of faith. Rooted in My grace, the fruit brings glory to Me and joy to you.

Lowliness comes as you confront your own nature and weakness. Pride falls as you see with undeceived eyes just who and what you are apart from My sustaining grace: loveless, totally self-consumed, critical and envious of others, fearful and ready to accuse. Not a pretty picture. But for this soul, your soul, My child, I was willing to die.

September Eighth

Then Job answered . . . I have heard of Thee by the hearing of the ear, but now mine eye seeth Thee. Wherefore I abhor myself and repent in dust and ashes.

Job 42:1,5,6

The time of trial reveals the true condition of your soul. Its weaknesses are displayed to view and your lack of preparation is manifest. Therefore trials are necessary if you are to grow and progress in your life with Me.

There is a healthy weakness which Job had to learn before Me. Your human weakness before My divine majesty will always be a part of your reality. But there is an unhealthy weakness which seeks excuses for disobedience and sin. This you must be more careful to recognize and overcome. You *can* overcome this in the right way by willing help and cooperating with My will. When your will is in harmony with Mine, no power can resist or defeat you. That should be incentive enough to spur you on in this necessary battle.

September Ninth

He that dwelleth in the secret place of the most High shall abide under the shadow of the Almighty.

Psalm 91:1

Mine indeed are the sheltering arms of love. Although you cannot see or recognize them, they are there. Faith, the faith that moves mountains and opens closed doors, sees them and rejoices.

In the past you have doubted and lost sight of My sheltering arms. Your pain, fear, and confusion blotted out the reality of My providence. The suffering you underwent was in large part your own making. But I did not despise or reject you in your darkness—and My arms were still sheltering and protecting you. Look back with new eyes, and see. Rejoice and give thanks until you are so grounded in Me that nothing will be able to shake you internally from this reality. Mine indeed, My child, are the sheltering arms of love.

September Tenth

Looking unto Jesus the author and finisher of our faith; who for the joy that was set before Him endured the cross, despising the shame...

Hebrews 12:2

Yes, My child, the cross is a bitter thing. It was bitter for Me when I bore it for you. You can never know how bitter it was, and you will never have to taste the full extent of its bitterness, because I bore it for you. Nevertheless, you must taste your part of its bitterness if you would be Mine.

All My children have their part in this saving process—and come away cleansed and blessed. I came down from the cross a dead Body—lifeless, ruined and done as far as the powers of this world were concerned. But a deeper power had been challenged and did not know that on that very cross—that bitter cross—he was being unseated. So My victory beyond the cross is stamped on every cross I ask My children to endure. Because I live, no cross is as bitter as was Mine. So do not fear any cross—you cannot be destroyed by it—only cleansed and made more fit for life in My kingdom.

September Eleventh

But to him that worketh not, but believeth on Him that justifieth the ungodly, his faith is counted for righteousness.

Romans 4:5

My living water I freely give to those who seek My face to live. My grace is not confined to the worthy. Rather it is designed for those whose only claim is their unworthiness. I do not ask My children to grovel before Me. When you are convicted of your sin, when you become painfully aware of your human proclivity to the lower elements of your nature, what I desire is an inward turning to My light, My face. This is not to make light of your wrongness, but to make Light of it, turning darkness to light.

It is at this point My children often become confused and veer into desert paths of their own choosing. Condemnation and fruitless effort do not make saints. Pride waits to ride in behind these substitutes for saving grace. My glory is obscured behind the subtle and secret pride in the effort put forth to make up for the feeling of condemnation. Tread carefully here, that you do not fall into the trap—the empty cistern—when living water flows freely from My throne of grace.

September Twelfth

In the wilderness shall waters break out, and streams in the desert.

Isaiah 35:6

I am the Lord your God. Come to Me in the dew of the morning and find cleansing and refreshment for your soul. I know your nature, your thoughts and your actions. None are hidden from Me. Come to Me in the dew of the morning, and find cleansing and refreshment for your soul. You are a dry and thirsty land without My refreshing showers. You have no life in yourself. Deadness and emptiness are the fruit of *you*. But with Me, My dear child, is plenteous redemption. Showers of blessing are waiting to renew the dry and parched soul. Let them fall on you. Welcome them and *believe* in My goodness. Do not flinch from My judgments *nor* from My grace. Let Me be your hiding place, for in Me is plenteous redemption.

September Thirteenth

Blessed are the poor in spirit.

Matthew 5:3

Humble your heart before Me, My child, and let the poverty of your spirit make its plea to Me. Presumption has long been a prevalent sin in your nature and it is far from being eradicated. Your sense of impotent waiting is My weapon against this proud and haughty dimension in you. It is but a mild rebuke and is a guard against spiritual pride—the deadliest of all. When these delays come, do not lose heart. Repent of your impatience and humble your heart before Me.

September Fourteenth

I am persuaded that neither death, nor life, nor angels, nor principalities, nor powers, nor things present, nor things to come . . . shall be able to separate us from the love of God which is in Christ Jesus our Lord.
                                                                    Romans 8:38,39

I am the eternal One whose name is holy. I dwell in the high and holy place, and also with those who are humble in heart. Your afflictions are sent in mercy, My child, and were not designed to destroy you. Rather they are sent to humble and train you in godly trust. You have much still to learn, because you withdraw from Me in your fear and imagine yourself alone. O foolish one! Nothing can separate you from My love—not even your withdrawal. Only you suffer needlessly when you choose fear instead of faith. Learn, learn!

September Fifteenth

But these things are written, that ye might believe that Jesus is the Christ, the Son of God; and that believing ye might have life through His name.
                                                                    John 20:31

Have I not told you that I am doing a new thing? It still unfolds before you day by day, if you have eyes to see. The end is not yet. My plans extend beyond anything you can see or imagine, but I have alerted you to be on the lookout for them, so that you may know what they are when they come to pass.

Do not fret or worry over the necessary delays along the way. These "pauses" are also part of My design, and are occasions for the exercise of faith—victorious faith. I want more faith and less fear—more confidence and less complaining. You are a purchased people, a chosen race, and I want you to live and walk as those who "know the festal shout." O My dear people, rejoice in what I have done for you. Believe in what I am doing and will do in you—and live as children of light.

September Sixteenth

And be ye kind one to another, tenderhearted, forgiving one another, even as God for Christ's sake hath forgiven you.

Ephesians 4:32

My forgiveness must extend to every hurt and wrong you *feel* you have sustained. Unforgiveness will block the flow of My life, and will rob you of the blessing I want you to know. Let every hurt be an occasion of *learning* from Me how to forgive. Put down absolutely and resolutely all thoughts of "evening things up." Accept the pain of not being able to redress the situation. That, at its best, would only "heal the wounds of My people lightly." Let My healing touch the wound, and remember, My child, there are other wounded souls besides yours. Pray to see clearly, much more clearly than you now see, how you have wounded another. Let go the demand to be heard and accepted. Inasmuch as lieth within *you*, live peaceably with all. That is all I ask of you—and it is enough.

September Seventeenth

Know therefore that the Lord thy God, He is God, the faithful God, which keepeth covenant and mercy with them that love Him and keep His commandments to a thousand generations.

Deuteronomy 7:9

A word for today, a faithful word I speak, I who am faithful: My favor rests on those whose hearts are toward Me. My favor rests on those who tremble within at My word. It must never be taken for granted, for that would be to bring Me down or lift you up in the wrong way. My word is sharper than a two-edged sword. I pierce between soul and spirit, joint and marrow—beneath the rational and reasonable exterior and the depths from which actions come. Heed My word, My child. It is life and health to you—here and hereafter. It is vitally important that you not only hear, but heed what I am saying to you.

Holy, holy, holy is the Lord God of Hosts. I dwell in the high and holy place, and seek a dwelling place on earth among the lowly. I am grieved at the ingratitude which allows your heart to close itself from Me. I am merciful and full of compassion, but I am the Holy One. Lose no time in turning to Me, and learn to avoid the ways that lead to darkness and death. You were created for *life*. Embrace My life more fully today, My child.

September Eighteenth

I have no greater joy than to hear that my children walk in truth.
III John vs. 4

Out of the darkness of fear I invite you into the light of faith. Out of the darkness of self, I invite you into the light of My glory. When you turn your thoughts to *you*, you enter a dark, windowless room—a kind of solitary cell. Uncertainties plague you, every small pain gets magnified because of what it might become. Yet you are not in prison—except by your own choosing. The key that opens the door and lets the light of My presence flood your soul is *praise*. It is not "begging prayers" but "returning thanks" that turns the key.

It gives Me no joy to see My children in their own self-chosen darkness. This brings Me not honor or satisfaction. It was not for this that My child gave His life. It was to draw to Me a free people with changed hearts and joyful spirits. The work of redemption has been done. Why grovel as though the battle had not been won?

Out of your darkness, I invite you, My child, into My light. Where I am, there is light.

September Nineteenth

In God I will praise His word, in God I have put my trust; I will not fear what flesh can do unto me.

Psalm 56:4

My dear child, your doubting of My goodness is a sin and offense against Me. How can you doubt? How can you doubt after all the ways I have shown you My mercy? I have fed and clothed you, led you along a path that you did not know nor understand. I have guarded your home and dwelling—and your children. There is no end to My faithfulness. Yet you come cringing, fearing, and full of your petty sin. Wash you and make you clean! Put behind you all these doubts and fears and repent of *them*—for My love and My grace do not ebb and flow with the changing tide. Gird yourself for the tasks ahead, and do not flinch from them. I will supply your need day by day. Only believe and receive—and doubt no more!

September Twentieth

I have gone astray like a lost sheep; seek Thy servant; for I do not forget Thy commandments.

Psalm 119:176

The breaking you are experiencing is a necessary part of the process. The hardness of your heart is like a calcification, protecting you from the pain you feared, but shielding you from the tender darts of My love and My leading. This breaking process must proceed. You remember how tears came unbidden when you were young—and your pride caused you to reject them and the fruit they were intended to bear. Let this hardness go. Let Me break up the calcification, so that My healing can be complete.

September Twenty–first

Blessed is he whose transgression is forgiven, whose sin is covered.
Psalm 32:1

My child, accept My pardon for your many failures, and go on in My strength the length of your journey. Continue to give thanks for My provisions and My heavenly watchcare. Build on the solid rock of My sovereign grace, and never let yourself be moved from the foundation. Redeem the time, and be faithful unto death.

September Twenty–second

Be sober, be vigilant; because your adversary the devil, as a roaring lion, walketh about, seeking whom he may devour.

I Peter 5:8

Your heart and My heart must come to greater union. My heart is My love—steady and unwavering, the "firm foundation" of which you love to sing. Your heart is still unsteady, fraught with distractions too numerous to mention. The old man of self-love and self-interest still dwells there, where only I have sovereign rights.

Godly sorrow for *who you are* is an important ingredient in this battle, but I want you to know it *is* a battle, and one you have not yet won. No one else can win it for you, and, although I will supply all needed grace, I will not carry you through without the struggle you *must* exert.

It is the "little foxes" that destroy the fabric of your soul, and in these "little" skirmishes you *often* lose ground unawares. Be vigilant, child of Mine, be vigilant and fight!!

September Twenty–third

In all their affliction He was afflicted, and the angel of His presence saved them; in His love and in His pity He redeemed them.

Isaiah 63:9

My dear child, I have no delight in the suffering of My people. I allow it only for their eternal good. Blessed are those who turn to Me in their trouble, for I am a God of mercy and compassion. The valleys through which I call you to go need not frighten you. The shadows and darkness are only for a time. Let your faith grow strong when darkness comes. Faith will overcome where daylight cannot prevail. Suffering purges away the rank growth of self—if you let it do its work. There are two ways in which I turn it to good: by its pruning and by My healing. In both ways I bring blessing to My chosen ones.

September Twenty–fourth

Many are the afflictions of the righteous: but the Lord delivereth him out of them all.

Psalm 34:19

My dear child, be content with My love and be attentive to My correction. Know that they come from My fatherly care, the Shepherd's care for His sheep. Let them turn your heart and mind in My direction instead of your own willful way. I will lead you in the right paths, and refresh you by the still waters of comfort. Only do not despise My chastening nor be discouraged at My corrections. They are a necessary element in your spiritual growth and progress. Bless My name and My ways, even when they confound your understanding— *especially* when they confound your understanding.

September Twenty–fifth

I will be as the dew unto Israel.

Hosea 14:5

In the dew of the morning, I come down to refresh and revive your soul. In the light of the morning, I dispel the darkness of your mind. In the joy of the morning I dispel the sadness of your spirit. You do not make these things happen. They are My gift and My work in your soul. I am still doing "a new thing," and it is My will that you be blessed in it. Bless Me in your heart—sanctify My name within your heart. Turn aside from every wicked thought and seek Me more faithfully and more frequently as your day goes on. Weariness comes, not from fighting, but from surrendering to the blandishments of the adversary.

September Twenty–sixth

Rest in the Lord, and wait patiently for Him.

Psalm 37:7

Those who wait before Me here cannot be disappointed, for I, the Lord, keep My appointments. Waiting may seem tedious, even confusing to you, My child, but *think!* Consider how long I have waited for you. It is not my reluctance but the massive barrier of *thought-habit* which keeps our communication from starting more easily. Waiting and repentance are good companions at this point in your journey.

September Twenty–seventh

I beseech you therefore, brethren, by the mercies of God . . .

Romans 12:1

O My dear child, the wonders of My love encompass you on every side. As yet you do not see or recognize many of them because you still look on the outward appearance. Why are you afraid to look more deeply? Do you not yet know that My intention for you is love? You cannot fully and effectively minister My reality to others if you are still afraid of seeing My full purpose and embracing it. There is resistance still in your heart against the full expression of My will. And this resistance separates you from Me. We cannot walk closely together when you pull back—afraid, accusing, rebellious. O My dear child, by My past mercies I appeal to you—yes, I the Lord, *appeal* to you: trust Me and do not separate yourself from the fullness of My love.

September Twenty–eighth

Bringing into captivity every thought to the obedience of Christ.

II Corinthians 10:5

Put away, My child, the thoughts that distract your attention. Fix your heart and mind on Me, that you may hear what I have to say to you. When these diverting thoughts intrude themselves, send them away promptly without paying any attention to them. Return in heart and mind to Me, for I desire to hold fellowship with you. Yes, I know you are unworthy and unfit for this. I am acquainted with your faults, even better acquainted with them than you are. But you do not yet grasp the depth of My merciful heart. You have had glimpses of it, but still do not see the greatness, the largeness of My love. I came not to judge but to save, not to destroy but to bring life, not to parcel out little rewards but to call you to a living, loving, and therefore obedient relationship with Me. We still have far to go to reach *that* goal—but I haven't given up!

September Twenty–ninth

For He knoweth our frame; He remembereth that we are dust.
                                                        Psalm 103:14

My child, My child, your prayer is heard. I do not despise you in your need. I know your frame and am acquainted with all your ways. I want you to draw near to Me and keep fellowship with Me. I want you to know that I am always with you, even when you are least aware of My presence. I am not a God who is far off, but One who is near. You experience a sense of separation and loneliness because *you* ignore My presence and wander after empty clouds and vain thoughts. So return to Me, and *keep* returning, for I am with you to bless, not to curse; to save, not to condemn.

September Thirtieth

Hold up my goings in Thy paths, that my footsteps slip not.
                                                        Psalm 17:5

My dear child, My word to you today is this: Walk in My love, as I have loved you. My love lays down a safe path for your feet. You do not know the dangers that surround you on every side, but I chart a safe course through them, and bid you walk there. The path is clear, and will open moment by moment as you have need.

OCTOBER

Maltbie D. Babcock
1858–1901

This is my Father's world,
    And to my listening ears
All nature sings, and round me rings
    The music of the spheres.
This is my Father's world,
    I rest me in the thought
Of rock and trees, of skies and seas;
    His hand the wonders wrought.

This is my Father's world,
    The birds their carols raise,
The morning light, the lily white
    Declare their Maker's praise.
This is my Father's world,
    He shines in all that's fair;
In the rustling grass I hear Him pass,
    He speaks to me everywhere.

October First

The word which ye hear is not Mine, but the Father's which sent Me.
John 14:24

Yes, My child, My word is in you—hidden beneath your over-active, undisciplined mind. I am here, and you know it not. I am acquainted with all your ways and your thoughts. Yet you forget and ignore My presence. The way of the transgressor is hard, and your *forgetfulness* is that: transgression. You do not have to sin openly to transgress. My will and My majesty are transgressed by inward attitudes long before outward deeds express them.

I call you to a more careful regard. Watch the little foxes that destroy—like the worms in the stems of squash—unseen until the damage is done. You cannot serve God and mammon—the world spirit, the *self* spirit. My conditions are still the same: Take up your cross daily and come with me—not at a *safe* distance but close behind Me. *That* is the safe place.

October Second

I have declared unto them Thy name, and will declare it; that the love wherewith Thou hast loved Me may be in them, and I in them.

John 17:26

I will walk with you, My child, all the way. I do not forsake those who put their trust in Me, however weak and wavering their faith may be. Few, very few, are strong in faith. The effects of sin and rebellion linger on in the soul even after new life has begun. But I claim as Mine all that the Father has given Me, and I do not abandon those who are Mine.

Put away this faithless fear you have been entertaining. I will be with you. What is there to fear with Me at hand? Claim the promise, child, whenever these fears assail your mind! Turn the moment into a blessing by recognizing and resisting the adversary in *My* power. Be prepared to *be* a blessing and you will *be* blessed. I repeat again: there is nothing to fear with Me at hand.

October Third

And He marvelled because of their unbelief.

Mark 6:6

This is the day of miracles. My power and love will combine and My glory will be shown. Awaken your heart, be expectant, not reluctant, before My promise. I can do exceedingly abundantly above all you ask or think. You need to stretch your faith, My child, instead of nursing puny, negative doubts and fears. Faith still moves mountains—faith and prayer. Faith borne on the wings of prayer. This is what you need to practice—faith-filled praying, expectant, eager and confident praying. My heart is gladdened when My children pray this way. Don't be afraid of believing too much. Be afraid of limiting My work and cheating My glory by believing too little. I love to reward a chastened, believing heart, a faith that has been tried and not found wanting. Pray for such a faith and *I will* give it to you; and then it is yours to guard and use for My glory. Awaken, My child, awaken your heart!

October Fourth

Therefore whosoever heareth these sayings of Mine, and doeth them, I will liken him unto a wise man, which built his house upon a rock.
                                                                    Matthew 7:24

I am that Solid Rock. There is no other besides Me. I am the sure Foundation of all your life and hope. Your rock-like mind is not the Solid Rock. It is the rubble of years of misuse. Yet it is hard, and you often get "stuck" in it and think you are firmly standing on Me. O my dear child, I am so much greater than these little "chunks" of opinion you stand on so bravely and full of pride. Your rightness is not your salvation. I am your salvation, but you can neither live it out nor even realize it unless you are willing to lose—to lose. You will "lose face" in your mind but nowhere else. Work today on being willing to lose—not just outwardly, but inwardly, and with a good heart and spirit. It is not as hard as you think!

October Fifth

He hath not dealt with us after our sins; nor rewarded us according to our iniquities.

Psalm 103:10

No, My child, you are not worthy that I should come under your roof. My presence in you is not based on your worthiness but on My grace. I am He who "is full of compassion and of great mercy." Otherwise, My creation would long ago have been destroyed.

I am with you in your struggle against your fallen nature. I have redeemed you. I have called you by name. You are Mine. But your old nature will not fit in My Kingdom of love and righteousness. It is a twisted and perverted nature and must die. Daily deaths are part of this dying. Do not flinch from them. They are from Me.

October Sixth

Be watchful and strengthen the things which remain, that are ready to die; for I have not found thy works perfect before God.

Revelation 3:2

The lame and the lepers were healed in an instant. The healing and repairing of your soul takes longer. The fabric of your soul has been badly injured and marred. The works of Satan are evident in its tattered condition. You are unstable and disloyal to yourself and to Me. Take seriously the opportunities you have to "strengthen the things that remain." Consider the bitter fruit of your past rebellion— bitterness that continues on even today. Let that strengthen you to fight every rebellious impulse in you, and learn to fight with the weapons and strength I supply.

October Seventh

And being in Bethany in the house of Simon the leper, as He sat at meat, there came a woman having an alabaster box of ointment of spikenard very precious; and she brake the box, and poured it on His head.

Mark 14:3

My dear child, do not forget that I love you. Do not heedlessly trample on My love by doubting it or forgetting it. My love is a purifier of motives, the inner hidden workings of the heart. It does cleanse and burn and consume the lower passions of your nature when you keep it as a peculiar treasure and gift. Everything that I ask of you and everything that I allow to come into your life is rooted in My divine love. You cannot measure or understand or comprehend My love—but you can accept it in a way you never have. The woman in the Gospel reading had accepted My love. Simon had not. Where is the alabaster box of ointment in your life? Break it, My child, and be amply blessed.

October Eighth

But exhort one another daily while it is called "Today"; lest any of you be hardened through the deceitfulness of sin.

Hebrews 3:13

The breaking must continue. The hardness is not all gone. A soft and tender heart is what you need. You have calcified your heart for many years, and it is My will that this damage be undone. A person after My own heart is one whose heart is sensitive to the pain of others, not wrapped up in saving himself from pain and suffering. Seek that, My child, if you would come after Me. Hate the hardness that spares a momentary pain but inflicts greater pain on others without thinking about it. I will not fail you. You do not have to do it alone.

October Ninth

Ye are all the children of light, and the children of the day; we are not of the night, nor of darkness. Therefore let us not sleep, as do others; but let us watch and be sober.

I Thessalonians 5:5,6

As the morning light rises in the dawn, illuminating the waiting earth, so My light rises in the soul, quietly, gently illuminating the inner heart. Do not shrink from My light, My child, for without it you are doomed to dwell in darkness. My light brings life, even as it discloses the distortions and deformities that must be healed. I am He who makes the crooked straight, the Healing of that which is out of joint. My light and truth belong to the Day of My coming, and I call you to be a child of the Day.

October Tenth

Is not this the fast that I have chosen? to loose the bands of wickedness, to undo the heavy burdens, and to let the oppressed go free, and that ye break every yoke?

Isaiah 58:6

What do I require of you, My child? I lay on you no burden but that which belongs to your peace. My requirements may seem irksome to you. I know that they often do. But they are sent for your healing and growth, and to make you what you tell Me you want to be—a blessing to others. I do not deal with you in isolation, but with all the connections of your life. Together they form the matrix of My mercies, and I use them all for My purposes.

October Eleventh

Blessed be the Lord, who hath not given us as a prey to their teeth.
Psalm 124:6

Yes, My child, you have been snatched from the jaws of death more times than you can possibly know. I have been with you and you knew it not. My patience and My lovingkindness have been your salvation.

How often have you provoked My goodness with your willful blindness and refusal to heed! Yet My mercies are still over all my works, and I have not abandoned you to yourself. Yours has been a rocky, unstable road, and I know the pain you have experienced—much, but not all, brought on by yourself. Today I call you to accept and enjoy My merciful presence. I am with you, My child, so do not ignore My lovingkindness.

October Twelfth

Through faith we understand that the worlds were framed by the word of God, so that things which are seen were not made of things which do appear.

Hebrews 11:3

New every morning is My love for you. Let your love for Me be renewed in this meeting. Put the fears and shadows of the night behind you, and see Me in the unfolding of the day.

This world extends in time by My permission and My will. Ages and eons and epochs—these are but moments in eternity. I have created you and called you to live in eternity. You cannot grasp or understand what that means. But you can embrace My love anew every day—every moment you are given to live. In this way you are entering eternity even while confined in time. Do not waste these little moments—seek to be renewed in your love for Me. Redeem the time. Fight the battle of faith.

October Thirteenth

So Jonah arose, and went unto Nineveh, according to the word of the Lord.

Jonah 3:3

Come to My side where rivers of mercy flow freely. Cleansing and renewal are ever to be found here. Let your tears mingle with

Mine for all that is and has been amiss in your life. Let the tears be of sorrow and of joy. The three days spent in the deep were days of change for Jonah. Even though his nature and opinions still rose up, nevertheless he obeyed My voice and went to Nineveh with My word. I charge you, My child, to be a faithful bearer of My word. Do not allow your fear of the disapproval of others make you unfaithful. You cannot enter fully into My joy and strength unless and until you risk that disapproval in order to deliver My word as faithfully as you can. I tell you that I am your shield and great reward! You did not choose Me, but I have chosen you to be a bearer of My word. O My child, do not fail yourself and Me!

October Fourteenth

For the word of God is quick and powerful, and sharper than any two-edged sword, piercing even to the dividing asunder of soul and spirit, and of the joints and marrow, and is a discerner of the thoughts and intents of the heart.

Hebrews 4:12

My word is near. It is more sure than the beating of your heart. It is a fire to burn away the dross of folly in your soul. It is warmth to kindle a saving love. It is light to scatter the dark shadows of your fear-generated night. Rejoice in My word, for through it I raise you to your intended dignity as a child of God. Bow before it, for through it I show you the lowliness of your fallen state. Be a hearer,

My dear child, and a doer. Heed and obey the word I speak—and enjoy life abundant.

October Fifteenth

Why art thou cast down, O my soul? And why art thou disquieted within me? Hope in God, for I shall yet praise Him, who is the health of my countenance, and my God.

Psalm 43:5

I am the Lord your God. Look for Me in all that comes to pass today. View the circumstances as My will—and do not struggle against them. Be at peace within, My son, for I am He who brings the gift of peace. When you are sad within and do not understand your own emotions, you "dis-stress" yourself, and stay stressed inside when you could be resting in My goodness and love. My will for you is to seek and find a heavenly rest—a rest that goes beyond your outer circumstances and is not disturbed by them.

October Sixteenth

Thou shalt not be afraid for the terror by night; nor for the arrow that flieth by day.

Psalm 91:5

The night seasons, My child, are the seasons of battle. "Thou shalt not be afraid for the terror by night, nor for the destruction that wasteth at noonday." Others before you have endured the assaults of the enemy which came in the darkness. But in Me, darkness and light are both alike—for I am the inner Light which dispels the power of the outer darkness.

When you give ground to fearful thoughts and vain imaginations, you open the floodgates to your adversary. Your only recourse is to flee to Me. In this case, fleeing is fighting. You are no match for his wiles, and you need to stay very close to Me if you would know My victorious power. I will help you, but I will not force you to come to Me.

Remember, My child, your pride—your spiritual pride—is being dealt with in these night battles. You are not a hero—just a frightened child whom I love.

October Seventeenth

Whosoever cometh to me and heareth my sayings, and doeth them . . . is like a man which built an house, and digged deep, and laid the foundation on a rock.

Luke 6:47,48

My dear child, the Rock on which you build your hope must be Me alone. All other foundations and underpinnings will crumble and give way. You have not been aware of how false and weak some of your "underpinnings" are. I have assured you that I will not leave nor forsake you—yet you have so relied on these other foundations that panic replaced peace, and fear replaced faith. Do not waste these experiences. Do not repress the memory of them as you go on. It is My love and mercy that led you into and out of the circumstances, and My love and mercy will open new opportunities for you to reject the false foundations and choose this one firm Foundation—the Rock of Ages. Repent and believe the Good News.

October Eighteenth

Therefore with joy shall ye draw water out of the wells of salvation.

Isaiah 12:3

Thirst for the living water. Seek the living water. My life-giving water renews and restores. Do not be content, My child, with the polluted waters of this present age. Turn your mind to My word of truth, My Shepherd's voice, and I will give you an abundance you have never dreamed possible. Turn, turn from the distractions and toys that occupy your time and thoughts, that My word and My will may prevail. Seek the living water and be renewed.

October Nineteenth

For all the Athenians which were there spent their time in nothing else, but either to tell or to hear some new thing.

Acts 17:21

Truth is a spring of living water. It does not grow stale nor hackneyed, even though the verbal expressions may seem time-worn. Truth carries life-giving properties for the soul, and without these properties the soul languishes and shrivels. Cherish and hunger for truth, My child, for it shall make you free. Whether it be pleasant or bitter, its effect is health-bringing.

Many souls run shipwreck in their pursuit of *new* thoughts and ideas. They lose their devotion to the truth they have once known. They are fascinated and dazzled by the entertaining effects of newness and surprise. Be careful in your seeking to hold on to the truth that I have entrusted to you. Beware boredom, for it is a sign that you are seeking a false goal—something that will crowd out the good entrusted to you. Don't worry about being *original*. Let Me take care of that!

October Twentieth

He maketh peace within thy borders, and fillest thee with the finest of the wheat.

Psalm 147:14

Let this mind be in you—a mind like that of My Son—to seek My face and My favor above all earthly treasures. My goodness has never failed, the stream of mercy has never run dry. You have been fed with "the finest wheat" and you have been spared many sorrows. Forget not, My child, the signs I have given you of My loving care.

In this period of your life, I call you to greater faithfulness in turning from temporary fulfillments to a longer view of My will. No longer do you have to guess or wonder about what your future will be. A walk on the path I have laid out for you is your future. It does not ask for, nor require, heroics. Just a simple, day-by-day walk with Me.

October Twenty–first

Forbearing one another in love; endeavoring to keep the unity of the Spirit in the bond of peace.

Ephesians 4:2,3

My child, today is a gift of My love. Your very life is a gift of My love for you. I want you to live as a child of love. I want you to reflect that love in your relations with others. Since I am the Source and Giver of life, there is no shortage of supply. Only if you interpose your self-driven life in these relationships will the flow of My life be impeded. Make the day brighter around you by denying your darkness and letting My light shine through you. Today is a gift of My love. Live as a child of My love.

October Twenty–second

If ye then, being evil, know how to give good gifts unto your children, how much more shall your Father which is in heaven give good things to them that ask Him?

Matthew 7:11

Expect good and not evil at My hand, My child. Would you give your children that which would hurt or harm them? How much more is My love and mercy toward you! Expect good—that is the faith that moves mountains. That is the faith that unlocks closed doors. That is the faith that overcomes the world. Simple? Yes, My child, for your life turns on such simple truth. You either look to Me with expectant faith, or you look with accusing thoughts. You bring your needs, knowing from all your past experiences that My help does not fail. And in your asking, you choose whom you shall believe: the accuser or the Faithful One. It's that simple. Expect good and not evil at My hand.

October Twenty–third

Ho, every one that thirsteth, come ye to the waters.

Isaiah 55:1

By streams of living water, I lead you, My child. Thirsty and faint, you will find refreshment here. I am that water which gives new life, renewed vigor and fresh beauty to your soul. The waters of comfort are here. The cleansing of sin is here. Do not fear to see and recognize My uses of material water to convey the blessing of living water. Stoop down, and drink, and live.

October Twenty–fourth

Let us not therefore judge one another any more; but judge this rather, that no man put a stumblingblock nor an occasion to fall in his brother's way.

Romans 14:13

Your fickle and unsteady affection is a grievous fault. You *can* become more stable and steadfast if you will give up judging others harshly and yourself softly. You want to love Me with your whole heart? Then hear and heed what I say. The path to steadfastness involves crucifying your hard and unmerciful nature. Grace abounds for this to happen. Do not fear to let it come to pass.

October Twenty–fifth

And again I say, Rejoice!

Philippians 4:4

Enter into the joy of your Lord. Not just at the end of the journey, My child, but even now, amid the shadows and rough places of the road, there is joy for you if you will abandon the burden of sadness. I call for a joy-filled band—a people who know My heart. Yes, the world still lies in the corruption of rebellion, and millions of souls are in pain. Those who seek and find and follow the Narrow Way are still few. But they can be a joyful company—singing the songs of ultimate victory and daily help for every need. Enter into My joy, My beloved.

October Twenty–sixth

Why are ye so fearful? how is it that you have no faith?

Mark 4:40

This is My word for you today: Hear and fear not. Draw near and fear not. Be of good cheer and fear not. The winds and waves still obey My will—and that includes all the storms that arise in your life. If you will listen more carefully and obey more readily, you will not be terrified by the billows and waves of life. Keep faith with this secret place. Again I say, Keep faith!

October Twenty–seventh

The effectual, fervent prayer of a righteous man availeth much.

James 5:16

Think not that I have forgotten those for whom you pray. Think rather of the many signs that your way is known to Me. Embrace those you love, near and far, with the arms of love, prayer arms. Let My love flow through your prayers to bless. Truly I say to you, My love seeks an entrance into lives that are closed to My voice. My love seeks without violating the freedom I have bestowed. My love waits, and in the meantime, I call you to believe, to expect, to love, and to pray. That is a dignity and privilege I have bestowed on you. Do not despise it, My child.

October Twenty–eighth

Great peace have they which love Thy law; and nothing shall offend them.

Psalm 119:165

With My peace I bless those who seek it. It is found in unexpected places and times, for it is not a peace as the world knows it. My peace is found in surrender. To the extent that you agree with My will, you realize that peace. It may be in the midst of uncertainty, even of pain, but when your will is united with Mine, peace follows. It cannot be otherwise.

Stress grows from your vain attempt to control your future. It comes from believing that you know the way you should go. O foolish one! I am the Way and I know the way. To surrender is to *give in* to My way over yours. Since My way is life and peace, does it not make sense to choose it? Great peace have they who love My way.

October Twenty–ninth

And many false prophets shall rise, and shall deceive many.
Matthew 24:11

I am truth and I am life. The words that I speak to you come with the nature of Truth. Never fear truth, My child, for it is life-giving and healing, even when it is most painful. Deception and delusions are ever ready to bend or twist the truth so as to destroy its effectiveness. Remember this: deception is death-dealing; truth is life-bringing. The song and the joy in your heart must always be grounded in the truth. Otherwise they are exercises in delusion and bring no life. I hear your prayers, My child, and I again assure you that your prayers will be and are being answered. Great things have yet to unfold in My purpose. It is My grace to allow you to witness them and share in the faith-fulfillment they are intended to bring. Open your heart, then, to My truth and My life.

October Thirtieth

Cast thy burden upon the Lord. Take My yoke upon you . . . for My yoke is easy and My burden is light.

Psalm 55:22 and Matthew 11:29,30

Cast your burden upon Me, and take My burden upon you. Your burden is too heavy for you, My child. It is laden with sins past, old guilt, many fears, and unwholesome ambitions. There must be a daily "casting" of this burden upon Me, or it will grow heavier and heavier, weighing you down and hindering your journey. Ask My Spirit's searchlight to show you where you need to face any sin, repent, and be freed.

Take My burden in place of yours. My burden of care, of love for others who may never return yours in kind, of faithfulness in prayer and the burden of faith, of *believing* where you cannot see. Accept *this* burden, My child, and travel light!

October Thirty-first

From the rising of the sun unto the going down of the same the Lord's name is to be praised.

Psalm 113:3

From the rising of the sun to the going down of the same, My name is praised by My people. But My name is blasphemed every day and every hour by those who do not know nor fear Me. Pray, My child, for those you love who are in the bonds of darkness. You are a vital link in their journey into light. Their fate is not sealed, but open to the possibility of repentance and change. I will not force them against their will, but prayer is a powerful force to bring against the gates of hell. It is the secret weapon that the enemy cannot ultimately destroy nor defeat. Keep hope in prayer, and believe, My child, that My love for them is greater than yours. My compassion knows no limit—no matter how disgusting or impossible their condition may appear to you. So keep praying!

NOVEMBER

Breathe through the
  heats of our desire
  Thy coolness and Thy balm;
Let sense be dumb, let flesh retire,
  Speak through the earthquake, wind and fire,
O still small voice of calm.

John G. Whittier
1807-1892

November First

There is therefore now no condemnation to them which are in Christ Jesus, who walk not after the flesh, but after the Spirit.

Romans 8:1

Know this, My child, there is no condemnation to those whose trust is in Me. My righteousness covers the wrongness that belongs to your old nature. My sacrifice of Myself is your "ticket" to heaven— not any rightness of your own. You still flinch and draw back when confronted with the "badness" of what your human nature is without My intervening grace. You still struggle to find evidence of "goodness" in yourself, and this becomes bondage instead of freedom.

Relax and let go. I am still with you. Do not try to reason everything out, but trust in My mercy.

November Second

And when Jesus saw her, He called her to Him, and said unto her, "Woman, thou art loosed from thine infirmity."

Luke 13:12

Take this day as it comes, as My gift to you and those you love. They are Mine, and My love for them is greater than yours. I know their inmost thoughts and their deepest wounds. I know where they have hardened themselves against further hurt. I am the Lord who heals. I am the repairer of breaches—the builder of ruins. Just as the woman was bound and bent with "the spirit of infirmity" for eighteen years, and could not walk straight, so My children become bound with troublesome spirits of unforgiveness and hurt, and remain crippled until My freeing touch releases them to new life. Do not be surprised at My goodness. Do not blink at the way I achieve My purpose. Trust in Me, O ye of little faith, that My promises will be fulfilled. Take this day as it comes. Rejoice, trust, hope—in Me.

November Third

You were sealed with that holy Spirit of promise, which is the earnest of our inheritance.

Ephesians 1:13,14

My gift to you is My indwelling Spirit. With no conscious awareness on your part, I dwell within, because you have been sealed unto the Day of redemption. I am gathering unto Myself a people to dwell eternally with Me. Even now that dwelling is prepared, and your life span is preparation to fit you for it. By My Spirit's indwelling, a work of training, pruning, cleansing, and nourishing is going on in your soul, so that when I raise you up, you will be prepared for the joys I have prepared. Do you see, My child, how My mercy covers *all* that happens, and that I am *never* far from you?

November Fourth

For my thoughts are not your thoughts, neither are your ways my ways, saith the Lord.

Isaiah 55:8

Yes, My child, My mercies are beyond numbering, and they are new every morning. It is My pleasure to do good things to My children and for My children. Just as you desire good for yours, I seek good for Mine.

My ways are not your ways and thereby you often become confused. You think of me as one like yourself—but My love is a pure love, not contaminated with self and sin and guilt as is yours. So, as My love and My ever-new mercies operate in your life and the life of your loved ones, learn to *entrust* them and yourself to My tender care. Only then can you know the "peace that passes understanding," for your peace will not depend on your understanding.

November Fifth

Be still, and know that I am God: I will be exalted among the heathen, I will be exalted in the earth.

Psalm 46:10

Be still. For in the stillness My Voice can be heard. I have brought you here for My purposes. Listen for My Voice and My guidance. Put aside your own preferences and reasoning. *Listen*, so that My purposes may prevail.

I enter your thoughts as light enters darkness. Without sound or fury, all becomes different. What was hidden is revealed, truth replaces error, reality replaces fantasy. Seek this grace, so that you will not stumble and lead others astray. My word and My will are worth seeking, and when found, they are worth following, at any cost.

Remember always, My child, I seek your good. My will for you is good. Despise not My ways, for they are the Way to life, peace, hope and joy.

November Sixth

Ye are a chosen generation, a royal priesthood, an holy nation, a purchased people; that ye should show forth the praises of Him who hath called you out of darkness into His marvelous light.

I Peter 2:9

I make the light of My countenance to shine upon you. I look upon you with mercy and compassion, because I know who you are. Look on yourself not with disdain or despising. You are the work of My hands, and too much negative attention on your failures and faults is an exercise in self. There is a better way—rejoicing in My saving work, rejoicing in what I have accomplished for you, rejoicing in My incarnation and My complete identification with you. I became what you are without sinning, in order to lead you toward what you are yet to be. The light of My countenance still shines upon you, and the path before us still leads to your true destiny. So do not whine or repine. *Rejoice* in Me, and all I have given you.

November Seventh

With good will doing service, as to the Lord, and not to men: knowing that whatsoever good thing any man doeth, the same shall he receive of the Lord.

Ephesians 6:7,8

You are still too concerned about what others think of you. This is a serious block in your relationship with Me. It distorts your perception and hobbles your feet. I would not have you to be unmindful and deaf to what others say to you, but you magnify their input to such a degree that it does not do its intended work. You are seeking life in their good opinion of you and you interpret their negative words as destruction rather than helpful correction of some fault.

This, My child, is immature behavior. Part of your hidden design in all your work is the demand that it be accepted and approved. Take courage and trust Me. I will not fail you!

November Eighth

*Now the God of peace, that brought again from the dead our Lord Jesus
. . . make you perfect in every good work to do His will.*

Hebrews 13:20,21

Serve me with gladness, My child, and rejoice in My mercy. Wait for Me when I bid you wait, and do not let your impatience betray you into disobedience. Faithfulness often involves waiting during quiet or dry seasons.

Purify your heart from hatred and bitterness. Purge out the leaven of desire for that which I have held from you. Self-pity has no place in our relationship. Serve me with gladness. *Rejoice* in My mercy. This is the path of true fulfillment, and you have the privilege of *choosing* it.

November Ninth

. . . that your love may abound yet more and more.

Philippians 1:9

My dear child, My thoughts are not like your thoughts, and My ways are not like your ways. That old truth is being underlined during this phase of your earthly journey. Your thoughts are erratic, moved by fear at the slightest shadow, ever ready to excuse yourself. By now you should know and accept that about yourself. When you are confronted with conflicting thoughts, especially about yourself, I counsel you to listen, to pray and to refuse to retreat into a stronghold of righteousness. Only in this way can you allow the truth further entrance into your soul. Only in this way can your thoughts align themselves with Mine. That, My dear child, is My aim and desire for you.

November Tenth

The Lord hath prepared His throne in the heavens; and His kingdom ruleth over all.

Psalm 103:19

In My will for you there is much still to be learned. The horizons of your mind are still too narrow and confined. Your heart must become larger and freer if you are to follow My plan for you. I have allowed you to see some of the vastness of My creation and to see the results of My patient process in creation. Let these images challenge the smallness and pettiness that is natural to you. Come out of the rigid narrowness of your nature and indulge yourself in the greatness of Mine.

My plans for you are not yet fulfilled. Embrace each day with a new enthusiasm and hope. Fight against the fear and negative outlook that lurks beneath the surface of your most positive days. My kingdom *will* come and My will *shall* prevail—so live and pray with a new confidence. This is pleasing in My sight—and more pleasing by far than cringing, fearful prayer that doubts My fatherly care!

November Eleventh

For whosoever exalteth himself shall be abased; and he that humbleth himself shall be exalted.

Luke 14:11

When you seek My glory, you seek your own good. When you seek glory for yourself, you seek your own hurt. My glory I will not give to another, for that would be a betrayal of Myself and the world I have made. But I am not such a one as you. My glory I share and shed on others when they are ready for it and open to it.

Seek My glory. Seek to honor Me and be very careful *not* to seek honor for yourself, even from those close to you. Accept as your cross—your healthful and saving cross—the *lack* of honor you experience. Remember who you are, My child, the good and the bad. And you will, with My help, be able to put to death your craving for honor and glory. When you seek My glory, you seek your own good.

November Twelfth

That we henceforth be no more children, tossed to and fro, and carried about with every wind of doctrine . . . whereby they lie in wait to deceive.

Ephesians 4:14

Put aside your petty thoughts and ways, My child, and allow your soul to be enlarged before My greatness. There are many mysteries you cannot understand for you are finite, dust. Yet I have loved you and called you forth from nothingness to share My glory and My love. This mystery will always remain a source of joy and wonder.

Do not try to reason out how My purposes unfold. Keep close to the central truths you have been shown, and do not wander into vain speculations. Remember that you are dust, and remember, My child, how vulnerable you are to temptation. Let no pride nor delusion of strength deceive you about your true condition. Your struggles are not over, and your mind easily moves into harmful areas which bring doubt, fear, and guilt.

I want you to come to a settled peace in Me. It can happen. You must seek this and be willing to cooperate with Me if it is to be yours.

November Thirteenth

Nevertheless the foundation of God standeth sure, having this seal, The Lord knoweth them that are His.

II Timothy 2:19

I have spoken to your fear and to your faith. I have laid a sure foundation on which to walk and stand. My foundation is sure—it cannot fail because it is Mine. Too many times, My child, you have stepped aside and stood on false foundations. When they gave way and betrayed your trust, fear grew in you. Now that your eyes have been opened and enlightened, you can choose to remain upon that Solid Rock which cannot fail. Build there and you will have nothing to fear when the storms come.

November Fourteenth

For God, who commanded the light to shine out of darkness, hath shined in our hearts, to give the light of the knowledge of the glory of God in the face of Jesus Christ.

II Corinthians 4:6

You are blessed, My child, when your mind is stayed on Me. When you allow your mind to wander in forbidden paths, thorns and pain await you. I said "allow" because you must give your mind permission to wander in paths of darkness.

My light is ever shining. It is always available to My children. I do not withhold it from those who are willing to seek it and walk in it. So choose light rather than darkness. Choose life rather than death. Choose My peace rather than torment. You are blessed when your mind is stayed on Me.

November Fifteenth

I know, O Lord, that Thy judgments are right, and that Thou in faithfulness hast afflicted me.

Psalm 119:75

I, the Lord, try the hearts of those I love. The furnace of affliction burns away the dross of self-love, the overgrowth of worldly cares. Though it seems hard, even cruel, it is love in action. Few understand this, and many of My children allow themselves to become confused and bewildered when the afflictions come. The heart must be tried, because it is fickle and untrustworthy. Your affections are not pure, but are mixed with personal desires that have nothing to do with My will for you. So with these "severe mercies," I trim away and purge away—with your cooperation and assent. Nothing about these trials is automatic, for I do not force your will. Be aware, My child, of the quality of mercy in all your afflictions—emotional and physical. They are meant to free you of guilt, fear, and false goals.

November Sixteenth

Let us labor therefore to enter into that rest, lest any man fall after the same example of unbelief.

Hebrews 4:11

My child, do not despise My chastening and do not doubt My love. Bend your neck to My yoke, and do not resist My leading. I know the way that is best for you. You do not know the way. Left to yourself, you would wander far afield from My path, and so, in mercy, I check and turn. Be not dismayed at these turns in the road. Do not willfully push past them, but trust the processes that I am using for your good. Go over the lessons you have learned and remember how much you still need to grow in faith and trust in me. Blessed are those who persevere in this path and do not "kick over the traces" by which I would steer them. You can choose to "stay the course" I have set before you. Do not resist My leading and do not doubt My love.

November Seventeenth

My beloved is mine, and I am His . . . until the day break and the shadows flee away.

Song of Solomon 2:16,17

I am here. I am here for you. I wait to be gracious. I wait to touch your heart with My tenderness. "Majestic sweetness sits enthroned." You have as yet touched only the edges of My ways, the hem of My garment. Remember this, My child, I am the Savior. I did not come into your life and your world to condemn you. I came to save you, to call you out of darkness into My light.

Where I am there is light. Darkness flees before My face, and the darkness in you must flee and find no room if you are to dwell in My light. I call you to be a light-dweller and a light-bearer, and My grace is sufficient for you.

November Eighteenth

It is good that a man should both hope and quietly wait for the salvation of the Lord.

Lamentations 3:26

In quietness you shall possess your soul. In stillness you shall hear My voice. Strive to enter into My rest. Learn the secret, while you yet have time, of letting go. You still cling to the old ways of anxiousness and care. Your fears are grounded in this clinging, so you are bound rather than free, troubled rather than peaceful.

Do you not know, My child, that I am the Source and Giver of the peace for which you long? Seek that peace which is Mine, for in it you will be freed from the night demons of panic and terror. Claim the inheritance which is yours as My child, and do not despise My dealings. Let not your heart be troubled, neither let it be afraid.

November Nineteenth

For God hath not given us the spirit of fear; but of power, and love, and of a sound mind.

II Timothy 1:7

In mercy I come to you to renew your spirit. Life is My gift to you, not only your physical life, but the spiritual life I impart. All life is Mine. That is a mystery too deep for your understanding. What you can understand, My child, is that your life is My gift and continually comes from Me. So why the worry and fear? Why do you allow ground for accusation against Me? Have I not promised to be with you to the end? Have I failed you hitherto? Be more aggressive against these wicked thoughts when they come in the night. Reclaim what you have surrendered and recognize the enemy when he appears.

Life is My gift to you. Your life continually comes from Me. Don't waste it in faithless fears and wicked accusations.

November Twentieth

Pure religion and undefiled before God and the Father is this, To visit the fatherless and widows in their affliction, and to keep himself unspotted from the world.

James 1:27

I send you out from these quiet times to live out and prove the realities you meet here. Only in the press of the day and the needs of the night can you come to know that what I tell you here is truth. Otherwise it would become an escape into an unreal world of fantasy, cut off from your real life. That is certainly not what these quiet times are meant to be. They are organically connected with the whole of your life: all your struggles, relationships, and uncertainties, your temptations and your wounds. Use them more faithfully. Recall them to mind more frequently. Refresh yourself here at the fountain of life for the heat of the day, and return hither in heart and mind in the dry season. My grace is sufficient for you.

November Twenty–first

Then shalt thou delight thyself in the Lord, and I will cause thee to ride upon the high places of the earth, and feed thee with the heritage of Jacob thy father.

Isaiah 58:14

My dear child, I delight in those who find their delight in Me. I grieve for those whose delights are of this passing world. They will suffer great loss and rob themselves of many joys.

I call you to center your heart upon Me. Your failures and successes are not the goal of life. The true goal is to seek and find true life in Me.

I tell you again that I have loved you with an everlasting love. When fear and darkness come upon you, recall this word to your mind. Resist the accusations of the adversary that My grace is not sufficient for your needs. Oh, there is plenteous grace beyond your direst need. Am I not God? Let love cross out fear and be one of those who find their delight in Me.

November Twenty–second

Inasmuch as ye have done it unto one of the least of these My brethren, ye have done it unto Me.

Matthew 25:40

Interruptions are also of Me. Do not forget the parable of the priest and the Levite. Never let your predetermined agenda keep you from seeing My hand in the interruption. It is there, whether you recognize it or not.

November Twenty–third

And I will rejoice in Jerusalem, and joy in my people.

Isaiah 65:19

I, the Lord God, Maker of heaven and earth, delight to hold fellowship with My lowly creatures. My love created them and gave them life and breath. My Spirit quickened them into new life, to enable them to seek Me and find Me in the appointed time. Marvel not that such is the case, for it is the nature of love to seek the good and happiness of others. My delight can only be increased as My children find true joy and delight. My divine happiness, My joy, is increased by theirs. The joy that was set before Me on the cross was the sure faith-knowledge that My death would bring joy and delight to My children.

I do not seek craven servants, but joyful children. I do not find pleasure in fear-inspired service, though I accept it as a way-station toward maturity. When the fullness of love comes, our relation can be based on a mutual desire to bring joy to the other. Learning to see My design in purging out false dreams and aims is a step—a necessary step in the path to maturity. The tapestry of My plan begins to "make sense" as you view your life in this light.

November Twenty–fourth

For of Him, and through Him, and to Him, are all things, to whom be glory for ever. Amen.

Romans 11:36

Hear, My child, the word for today. There is no need that I cannot fill. There is no situation that I cannot redeem. Your faith is still dwarfed and stymied by your reasoning, and your deep fear is the product. Only by trusting Me beyond the limits of your reasoning can you begin to have freedom from the plaguing fears.

The future is Mine—your future and the future of your loved ones. My arm has not been cut off, and My resources are limited only by My nature and My will. I am aware of all your circumstances and the anxieties you entertain even in sleep about those you love. Be of good cheer. The end is not yet, and I am still at work. I have not forgotten My promises, and My plans for you are good, not evil. Stay on the path I have set before you, and trust Me for all that is to come.

November Twenty–fifth

Blessed be the Lord God of Israel from everlasting to everlasting: and let all the people say Amen. Praise ye the Lord.

Psalm 106:48

My child, your thankfulness gladdens My heart and strengthens yours. It truly is a *good* thing to be thankful, because gratitude aligns your soul with My Spirit and opens you to the healing streams of My mercy. My heart is always gladdened when any child of mine becomes open to My mercy. Gratitude opens the "channels of reception," which are necessary for you to receive the blessings I would willingly pour out on you. Gratitude is an antidote to false pride and its distortions of the soul. It is an antidote to fear, because the soul recognizes the benevolence and good will which lay behind the gift. Gratitude opens the channels of fellowship and charity, because it kills false competition and jealousy. I have called you many times to praise and give thanks. My Word exhorts My people to give thanks. These are some of the inner reasons why praise is essential for your life with Me. Praise opens clogged channels, and the soul can grow stronger in the purer sunlight of My love and goodness when it turns away from itself and exercises this holy privilege.

Yes, My child, your thankfulness gladdens My heart and strengthens yours.

November Twenty–sixth

Thou compassest my path and my lying down, and art acquainted with all my ways.

Psalm 139:3

I am the first and the last, the beginning and the destiny of your life. I called you into being out of nothing, and willed your existence on earth. I loved you, even before you were conceived in your mother's womb, and planned the path of your earthly life. I took into account your nature and the wrong choices you would make. They could not defeat My power and My plan, but they would cause you grief and suffering. My will for you is life, health, and strength. Weakness and sickness are *allowed* but are not My perfect will. Nevertheless they are useful in fulfilling My plan. My persevering grace has kept you from falling headlong into ruin. Repentance and praise now are necessary to advance in the path I have set before you. Praise *is* repentance for it is a recognition and acceptance of My way over yours. Go forward along that path, for I am with you.

November Twenty–seventh

When He putteth forth His own sheep, He goeth before them, and the sheep follow Him: for they know His voice.

John 10:4

My voice is a mighty voice. My voice is a still, small voice. I speak in tones designed to carry out My will. Your ear is still too much attuned to your own voice and the voice of the world. Silence is essential to tuning in to My words to you. Do not think the time wasted in waiting. Do not grow impatient or disheartened that it takes you so long. Remember how long you have lived without this necessary preparation—and how sporadic and scattered were the times you "heard" My voice. I have had to speak in "loud" tones of circumstances—some of them drastic—to guide you in My chosen way. But I would prefer to speak in the still, small voice, and see you willingly hear and obey. So I bid you, My child, do not give up on your waiting and listening—and learn to be still and know My voice.

November Twenty–eighth

He upbraided them with their unbelief and hardness of heart.

Mark 16:14

Yes, you are fearful to open the door of your heart to My voice. You are afraid of what I will say about your sins. And so this delay in our communion, while you "dance about," insisting that you want to hear My word to you. You are still divided and pride still rules where humility should reign. O proud and foolish one! How long will you linger in the shades of separation when we might be walking together in the path of light? I am grieved at your slowness of heart. I appeal to you by My many mercies—give up this´ pride and get on with it!

November Twenty–ninth

. . . that in me first Jesus Christ might show forth all longsuffering, for a pattern to them which should hereafter believe on Him to life everlasting.
I Timothy 1:16

I am the God of mercy. Your life, My child, is a manifestation of it. You have not chosen Me, but I have chosen you, and set My mercy upon you. In a vessel such as you are—weak, unstable, hidden, and high-minded—only My mercy can bring forth any lasting good. The unlovable elements in your nature work against that mercy—war against it—striving for ascendancy and recognition. They are *always* self-defeating. They produce their own punishment. *But* My mercies fail not. And your life is meant to show the fruit which grows from both. Let mercy prevail!

November Thirtieth

As long as I am in the world, I am the light of the world.

John 9:5

Morning by morning I speak to your heart. Morning by morning I renew your hope. The darkness of night is dispelled by the light, and the darkness of self is dispelled by My light. There is no life without My light—and whenever you choose your own way, you walk in the darkness of death. Joy and gladness do not—cannot—live in that self-chosen darkness. Fear and foreboding warn of the danger ahead if you persist in it. Seek the light, My child, seek the light.

DECEMBER

I am thine, O Lord,
  I have heard Thy voice,
And it told Thy love to me;
But I long to rise in the arms of faith,
  And be closer drawn nearer to Thee.
Draw me nearer, nearer, nearer blessed Lord,
  To the cross where Thou hast died;
Draw me nearer, nearer, nearer blessed Lord,
  To Thy precious, bleeding side.

Fanny J. Crosby
1820-1915

December First

But his word was in my heart as a burning fire shut up in my bones, and I was weary with forbearing, and I could not stay.

Jeremiah 20:9

My word is a fire—a purging, purifying fire—burning the dross and refuse of the years past. My word destroys as well as it builds. It must destroy strongholds of darkness and rebellion. You do not even know where or what some of those strongholds are in your soul. They must be assaulted and destroyed that you might be whole in Me. My word is not always in words. My word is My will going forth from Me to accomplish My purpose. You may tremble or weep before it without consciously knowing why or what is being done. Do not worry. Submit yourself inasmuch "as lieth in you" to My sovereign purpose. Keep silent before My mysterious ways, for all will be light in the end. Faith requires this, to trust where you are mystified, to hold on to what I have said when the outward conditions seem to contradict it. This is the way and walk of faith.

December Second

Thou shalt show me the path of life; in Thy presence is fullness of joy; at Thy right hand there are pleasures for evermore.

Psalm 16:11

Draw near to Me, and I will draw near to you. I am ever near, but you are usually unmindful of it. It takes a conscious choice on your part to enter into a realization that I am here.

My aim and purpose for you, My child, is for you to dwell in My presence. In My presence there is fullness of joy. In My presence is peace that passes understanding. But in My presence there is no room for self-absorption and self-promotion. These things must die and be purged away. They are deadly and death-giving. They must die so that *life*, true life, My life, can be yours.

Bless the means by which I further My plan for you. Keep before your eyes what I have told you. In My presence there is fullness of joy.

December Third

Casting all your care upon Him, for He careth for you.

I Peter 5:7

Cast your burden upon Me and I will sustain you. I am He who bears the burden of the weak. You have not yet learned the secret of

My burden-bearing, and you inflict pain on yourself and others in your reaction to situations you feel are unjust or unfair. You still demand that others think of you the way you think of yourself, and in your determination not to come under their "false accusations," you strike or lash back. My dear child, you do not have to do this! You are a sin-bearer, and I am ready to enter the situation "with healing in My wings" if you will cast your burden upon Me. Your way has never worked—so why not try Mine?

December Fourth

We are His people and the sheep of His pasture.

Psalm 100:3

I know My sheep and call them by name. This is a mystery beyond your comprehension, for you rightly see how impossible it is for the human mind. But I am the God of the impossible—by which I mean that My power and ability far exceed any thought you might have of Me—however grand and majestic it might be. In My choice to become man and dwell among you, I did not diminish My infinity. Your life has been too circumscribed by your mental boundaries. You have severly limited your participation in My divine greatness by these boundaries. But hear this word again and meditate on it. It contains a key to unlock resources you have not dreamed of or yet experienced. I *know* My sheep and call them by name. My dear child, that little word can make all the difference—if you learn to believe it.

December Fifth

These are they which follow the Lamb whithersoever He goeth. . . .
Revelation 14:4

As the eagle flies upward, above the noise and strife of this busy world, so should your soul "fly upward" to commune with Me. Most of your life has been lived in the lowlands—your thoughts and imaginations—even your dreams—have lodged there. Take this invitation seriously, My child, while there is yet time. Do not worry about what others are doing or thinking—for that is but a weight and hindrance to you. Seek My face. Seek to know Me in Myself—not hearsay or opinion—but a living knowledge that I will impart, if you will "follow the Lamb wheresoever He leads." Be bold in your need and do not fear to draw near.

December Sixth

For the vision is yet for an appointed time, but at the end it shall speak, and not lie; though it tarry, wait for it; because it will surely come, it will not tarry.
Habakkuk 2:3

Think not that your prayer is wasted, no matter how long the wait. Remember what I have told you, and keep on praying. You do not know the "ins and outs" of what is being done with your prayer in the meantime. I call for faithful perseverance through the cloudy and murky times, when you cannot see any answer coming. It is in this time that your love for Me grows in the secret place. Trust My unfailing love and My sure word of promise.

December Seventh

We love Him because He first loved us.

I John 4:19

As I have put it in your heart to seek Me, so it is in My heart to seek you. I speak in human terms so you can grasp the *living-ness* of My love and care for you. You are not an orphan, even though you have "orphaned" yourself by denying who you are. Your sins past and present are ways of accomplishing that. Thus My seeking—again I speak as a man—finding ways and circumstances to bring to your mind and heart who you are and where you are. Yes, it is I who move you to seek Me, and I will not rest until it has been accomplished!

December Eighth

The devil is come down unto you, having great wrath, because he knoweth that he hath but a short time.

Revelation 12:12

Come with Me, My child, into the future I have prepared for you. The years and the ages are Mine, and I am a safe Guide and Companion.

The past is covered by My redeeming sacrifice. It lives in your memory to be a perpetual reminder of your sinful nature and My grace. You have seen how I have moved to redeem that which was beyond your control, and what I have done, I am still able to do.

This world, in all its brokenness and darkness, is still the world for which I laid down My life. The enemy is still not convinced that My victory is complete, so with great wrath he snatches whomever he can. Prayer is a mighty weapon against his power. Do not forget this. Prayer *does* make a difference, because I have made a place for it in My divine plan. So keep praying as My Spirit directs and leads—and do not forget My little ones. O do not forget My little ones!

December Ninth

So being affectionately desirous of you, we were willing to have imparted to you, not the gospel of God only, but also our own souls, because ye were dear to us.

I Thessalonians 2:8

My child, grieve not over the things that are lost to you. Strengthen the things that remain. I have taken nothing from you that is of eternal value. I remove in order to fulfill. I take away that I might give. My way is always to supply what you need in abundance, even when that abundance feels like deprivation.

My generosity to you is commensurate with My mercy. It is never-failing and always in right proportion. So there is no cause for worry or anxiety, but much cause for gratitude and rejoicing.

I note your sense of loss in relationships—and say again to you: Grieve not over those who are lost to you. They are not lost to Me nor to My divine mercy. Rest in the assurance that I am faithful and know what is best. That for you can be a place of settled rest.

December Tenth

Moses said, I will now turn aside and see this great sight, why the bush is not burnt.

Exodus 3:3

It is My delight to see My children seeking My face. Seek and you shall find. Knock and it shall be opened to you. I am found by those who seek, ask, look—and I *never* turn away any sincere soul.

Wonders are commonplace compared with the souls that truly seek My face. For this reason, you are likely to become a little "peculiar" in the eyes of others—even those close to you. Turning aside to the burning bush, listening for My voice, obeying My commands—these all set you apart from what is considered ordinary and normal. But you must not allow this privilege to make you special in your own eyes. Rather let it make you more aware of how utterly dependent you are for daily strength and for wisdom to decide between good and evil.

Bring your hurts and your sins here, My child. The "throne of grace" is open to you—and to all who seek My face. Give up defending yourself—learn from Me—and seek My help in overcoming this fault.

December Eleventh

Beloved, now are we the children of God, and it doth not yet appear what we shall be: but we know that, when He shall appear, we shall be like Him; for we shall see Him as He is.

I John 3:2

Blessed indeed are you, My child, to be called into the fellowship of the redeemed. Happy, thrice happy, are those who forsake their ways and follow Me. My plan of redemption encompasses the beginning, the middle, and the end. Along the way the discarded ways are left behind. The dreams and ambitions fade, shrivel, and die. The sins are revealed, and repented, and forgiven. The rebellions are quelled and the wars cease. This must all take place before the full happiness to which I have called you can be experienced.

Yes, I have called you to "happiness"—by which I mean the cup of joy, the internal harmony and peace, and the full realization of My love, which as yet you but dimly see. On such a case as yours I set My love and prove again that I am conqueror over the fall. The price is high, but I chose to pay it, and choose to carry it to final victory in souls like yours.

December Twelfth

Wherefore I put thee in remembrance that thou stir up the gift of God, which is in thee by the putting on of my hands.

II Timothy 1:6

The fire of your love is smoldering beneath the years of neglect, bitterness, and rebellion. Your proud and stiff neck did not bend willingly to the yoke I laid on you. The circumstances were beyond your control, but you made choices in reaction to them. As a result, the little flame which had been rekindled sputtered and all but died out. Only My grace prevented that from happening. But now you live with the consequences of your resistance to My will. The work of restoration is not complete. I have given you the gift of tears to soften the hardness you have built up—and that is a start. But you must root out the bitterness and cynicism—they will not be "taken" away from you. *You* must throw them out. With each decision on your part to *accept* My will without bitterness, your altar fire will burn more brightly, and I will not fail to bless.

December Thirteenth

When He, the Spirit of truth, is come, He will guide you into all truth;
for He shall not speak of Himself; but whatsoever He shall hear, that
shall He speak; and He will show you things to come.

John 16:13

My Spirit I have given to *lead* you into all truth. Do not be surprised that you have had to "change your mind"—because I have continued to deepen and enlarge your tiny, shallow faith over the years. You have traveled a crooked path—setting off in your own direction over and over again. But My grace has not failed you. "Through many dangers, toils and snares you have already come." You know them only in part—and have little awareness of *how* dangerous some of those "detours" were for you.

As My grace has not failed you, you can count on it for those you love. Your fears are rooted in guilt and the desire to be loved by them. Cast away both and throw yourself into the ocean of My merciful love—and be at peace in your prayers. My plans far exceed your own and even a glimpse of them can fill your heart with "joy unspeakable and full of glory."

December Fourteenth

. . . I have set my face like a flint, and I know that I shall not be ashamed.
Isaiah 50:7

My word to you today is: Stay. Stay on the course I have laid out for you. Stay your mind and thoughts on Me. Stay within the bounds of My will, and you will know My peace. Stay by Me in prayer and thanksgiving. Stay with My word, which is able to keep you from being led astray in strange paths. Stay the hand of the wicked one with prayer. Stay the course. Finish your race with joy. I will not leave you alone. I *will not* leave you alone. Banish such thoughts and fears, knowing whence they come.

December Fifteenth

I will make darkness light before them, and crooked things straight. These things will I do unto them, and not forsake them.
Isaiah 42:16

The images of your children are etched deeply in your memory. How much more are Mine etched in My heart! My wrath and My mercy are one—and both are meant to turn people to the saving path I place before them. Perfect, mature love casts out fear. When the heart is secure in Me, there is no ground for fear of My wrath.

Learning the height and depth of My love for you is a life-long process. You have not chosen Me, but I have chosen you, and ordained you that you should bring forth much fruit. You will not see much of that fruit in this world, but My eye is upon it, and My will is carried forward through it. Marvel not at this. "By feeblest agents" does My righteous will get accomplished. Let My will bless you, My child, and take heart.

December Sixteenth

And I beheld, and I heard the voice of many angels round about the throne and the beasts and the elders; and the number of them was ten thousand times ten thousand, and thousands of thousands; saying with a loud voice, "Worthy is the Lamb that was slain to receive power, and riches, and wisdom and strength, and honor, and glory and blessing."
Revelation 5:11,12

More and more as you turn to Me, your time and thoughts should be spent in praise and thanksgiving. Heaven, after all, is a place of praise. There, with full vision, and understanding clarified, there is neither sorrow nor crying nor vain regrets—but praise filling every heart. As you give yourself to praise here, you enter the heavenly realm. Your praise, inadequate as it is, unites with that of the heavenly family—and is magnified in the process. "The humble shall hear thereof and be glad."

Take this thought, My child, and dwell on it. Your negative and fearful thought-life must be attacked on many levels—and none is more important than this one.

December Seventeenth

And it shall come to pass, that like as I have watched over them, to pluck up, and to break down, and to throw down and to destroy, and to afflict; so will I watch over them, to build, and to plant, saith the Lord.
Jeremiah 31:28

My child, the times and the time are in My hands. I am never late, and I keep watch on those who are Mine. The insignificant things that pass your notice are all part of My timing. I want you to become more aware of these small evidences that I put before you. They can strengthen your faith and trust in Me. Become aware of the *structure* of each day, for in that structure I am at work—for you and for everyone involved. Coming and going, present and absent—these are all part of that structure.

You wonder why I do not tell you more. Each "small" word carries the seed of change and growth—and I expect your cooperation in responding to each one. You could not fruitfully handle more than I am giving you. "Despise not the day of small beginnings"—just *begin*.

December Eighteenth

Wherefore, as the Holy Spirit saith, Today if ye will hear His voice, harden not your hearts.

Hebrews 3:7,8

My word to you is this: Today if you hear My word, do not harden your heart. The encrustation of self-defense is like corrosion on metal. It forms a protective and insulating barrier against the truth. In the meantime its corrosive effect is also at work, tearing down even the good that has already been done. This is why I said in the Scripture, "The latter state is worse than the first." The deadness, torpor, the inability to be inwardly moved—these are indicators that damage has already been done.

There is no sin that does a more deadly work to the soul than hardening the heart. So I say again, "Today if you hear My word, do not harden your heart. He that has ears to hear, let him hear."

December Nineteenth

And he [Paul] said, Who art thou, Lord? And the Lord said, I am Jesus whom thou persecutest: it is hard for thee to kick against the pricks.

Acts 9:5

My will is peace. Peace amid strife and peace growing out of strife. When your will is aligned with Mine and in harmony with

Mine, there is a settled peace that nothing can destroy. When your will is contrary, set on its own direction, there is no inward peace, however calm the outward circumstances.

The real strife—that which produces stress—comes from the lack of inward peace. The hypertension of My children is frequently related to this unresolved inner conflict. *Strive* to enter this rest, this "peace that passes understanding." Stay open to My truth, however it comes, and do not fight to have your own way. The price is too high for you, and the results are not worth what they cost.

December Twentieth

Grace be to you, and peace, from God our Father, and from the Lord Jesus Christ.

Ephesians 1:2

Freely have I forgiven you and freely have I accepted you in My heart. Your unbelief robs you of the peace My acceptance is designed to give you, and your doubt feeds and is fed by self-concern. Even your contrition over your lack of faith turns inward and bears no fruit. I keep telling you this because you continue to harbor the wrong kinds of doubts. Cleansing the inside of the cup involves throwing away—discarding—these empty and fruitless questions.

Keep praising My goodness and allow Me to lead you in your present relationships—that My purpose may yet be fulfilled.

December Twenty–first

Now there are diversities of gifts, but the same Spirit.

I Corinthians 12:4

The gifts I give may seem strange to you, My child. But they are expressions of My love and mercy. Sometimes I give the gift of suffering with Me—a privilege I offer to those who can bear it. You cannot understand this mystery with your natural mind any more than you can understand how My death on the cross can bring salvation to the world. But your spirit can affirm My goodness in what I bring or allow—for hidden within it all is the gift of My love.

Your gift-giving has a mixture of good and bad in it. You are interested in bringing joy and happiness to your loved ones, but you also know that your gifts fall wide of the mark. They can only bring pleasure for a season—and a pleasure mixed with dissatisfaction. I do not let such worries interfere with My gifts, because I know the end for which I give them is good and will work eternal joy in My children when they have accomplished their goal.

December Twenty–second

This grace is given, to make all men see what is the fellowship of the mystery, which from the beginning of the world hath been hid in God, who created all things by Jesus Christ: to the intent that now unto the principalities and powers in heavenly places might be known by the church the manifold wisdom of God, according to the eternal purpose which He purposed in Christ Jesus our Lord.

Ephesians 3:9–11

As you draw near to the commemoration of My birth, I want you to see why there is so little information given about its details. The human mind craves particulars. But My coming among you is a Mystery—and must remain wrapped in mystery if it is to convey its deepest truth. So do not be misled into thinking that more facts mean more truth. Let the mystery remain—and wonder.

December Twenty–third

In hope of eternal life, which God, that cannot lie, promised before the world began.

Titus 1:2

I am with you, My child, in all the circumstances you encounter. I am with you for good, and for your good. You need not fear the changes—but learn the blessing of childlike trust in Me.

What you call the "future" is all known to Me, and I work in the "present" to bring about My divine purpose. Small things and great—all fit into a pattern leading to My goal. Take care to be faithful. *Expect* answers to your prayers. You have not really begun to learn the power I have entrusted through *believing* prayer. I am the Source of all good things—and that includes "glad surprises" along the way.

December Twenty–fourth

Fight the good fight of faith, lay hold on eternal life, whereunto thou art also called.

I Timothy 6:12

This is My word to you today, My child. Keep diligently what I have committed to you. The time is short. The days are evil. Look for the manifestation of My glory. Put away childish ways—and let your faith in Me grow more childlike. Deny your desire for vindication and acceptance. Quell your appetite for place and power. Take a seat among the lowly—and there you will find sweet companionship with Me.

Remember, My child, that when I came to earth, it was in a stable that My mother gave me birth. Honor and love her—for her suffering and faithful patience. Let her be an example of the soul that finds favor with God. I still dwell among the lowly in heart. There you can always count on finding Me.

December Twenty–fifth

Having made known unto us the mystery of His will.

Ephesians 1:9

Quiet, My child! Be quiet before the Mystery. Silence becomes you as you think with awe on what I have done. My presence is an oasis of peace in this angry, troubled world. Mankind has yet to learn to be silenced before My Mystery. Eternity does not enter the thoughts of the angry soul. Let My haven of peace, the lowly stable, be a refuge from your anger and ambitions. Quiet, My child, and think on the Mystery of the ages—and be at peace.

December Twenty–sixth

For with thee is the fountain of life: in Thy light shall we see light.

Psalm 36:9

Look to the sunrise! Look to the day-dawn. Turn from the darkness, do not dwell on the shadows of the night. My glory is in the dawn. My way is open. There is light on your path—the light of truth and the sure word of My promise. O My child, rejoice in the light. Cast away dark thoughts and fear-laden burdens, and be a light-follower. Those who walk with Me shall not walk in darkness, but have the Light of life. Look to the sunrise!

December Twenty–seventh

For the Lord is good; His mercy is everlasting; and His truth endureth to all generations.

Psalm 100:5

The generations rise and pass away before Me. You see and experience sadness as your own generation draws nearer to the grave. Soon, very soon, you will all be forgotten by the living. Only a few from each generation are remembered. But I do not forget. These brief years on earth—with their sorrows, hopes, and joys—are not the whole of My gift of life.

I am the God of the living—and My gift of life goes on for those who come to Me for life. My care and My love do not end with the grave—so do not look with sad eyes at the brevity of your life here. Open them to the beauty of holiness and grace. Let these final years be both a finishing and a beginning—for My gift of life is an unending one for My own.

December Twenty–eighth

For from within, out of the heart of men, proceed evil thoughts, . . . All these evil things come from within, and defile the man.

Mark 7:21,23.

Child, the distractions of your mind are the fruit of your rebellion. For years you have thought that your mind is your private possession, not realizing that the adversary was using it as a "play-ground." You come to Me, desiring a quiet and settled dialogue with Me. You find instead a veritable crowd of extraneous thoughts and images seeking *and finding* entrance into your "side" of the dialogue.

Confess and yield up these contrary intruders quickly and return to Me. In quietness and peace you shall possess your soul. There is much work to be done here. Think soberly about these things if you really desire to go on with Me in these meetings. Do not imagine that you have progressed far in this. Remain keenly aware of where you are coming from and how far you have to go.

December Twenty–ninth

The Lord is good to all; and His tender mercies are over all His works.
Psalm 145:9

In My mercy there is provision for your every need. My ways seem strange to you, and sometimes you rebel against them. But in so doing, you are rebelling against My mercy.

A frightened bird can do itself much harm in trying to escape the loving attention of a well-intentioned person. Even so, you can bring harm to yourself in "kicking against the pricks" of My mercy when you don't recognize it.

This world calls such acceptance unreality, "Pollyanna-ish." But I call it a pearl of great price, a treasure hid in the field of your life— a trust like Mary's which allowed My purpose to proceed without hindrance or delay. Remember, My child, My *tender* mercies are over all My works. In My mercy there is provision for your every need.

December Thirtieth

The Lord shall preserve thee from all evil: He shall preserve thy soul.
Psalm 121:7

I will show you the way. You do not know what lies ahead, but I do. It will be well, for I will be with you. Waste no time in idle speculation or vain regret. Live today in My present, merciful love, for I am with you, My child—I am with you.

December Thirty–first

They said unto Him, Rabbi (which is to say, being interpreted, Master), where dwellest thou? He saith unto them, Come and see.

John 1:38,39

The way before you is a good way. You do not need to see the distant views, but keep your eye on the present choices. I have not called you to be a purposeless wasteland, but to be a fruitful field, to bear fruit for My kingdom. You do not need to know where or how this will come about. Your pride must not be fed in the process. But I will tell you this—you do not need to fear being left adrift or cast aside. Those are thoughts of self, and they have no place in our relationship. So be about My business. Put aside the murmurings of your old nature, your yearnings for gratification which you sought in "place" and "respect." Let go these things for My sake, and each time you feel a wound, bring it to me for forgiveness. Pride dies hard, so don't be surprised that it is still struggling for life in you.